Farm Girl

Edith S. Bailey

Farm Girl

by

Edith S. Bailey
1001 East Oregon Road
Lititz, PA 17543

ISBN: 978-1-60126-053-6
Library of Congress Number: 2007904111

All artwork on the cover and throughout this
book was hand-drawn by author Edith S. Bailey.

Printed by
Masthof Press
219 Mill Road
Morgantown, PA 19543-9516

This Book is Dedicated to . . .

my daughters,

Mabel Martin, Edie Martin and **Flo Good**

also

A special *Thank You* to everybody's friend,
John Fisher,
for his immeasurable patience as he taught this,
nearly, eighty-year-old woman to use the computer
for this story.

Table of Contents

Introduction

This is the story of an Old Order Mennonite family, the parents who had too much responsibility, and their offspring who had too little supervision and attention.

Most of these incidents actually happened as I remebered them, but the time frame may not be correct, as this is where my memory fades.

I wrote this story about 40 or 45 years ago when these incidents were still fresh in my memory.

I am now an 80 year-old mother to three daughters and three grandchildren. I still have two brothers and one sister living.

I hope you will enjoy reading this book as much as I enjoyed writing it. The Good Lord bless you and yours.

Edith S. Bailey

Chapter 1

Farm Girl

T he clanging of the milk cans as they were being loaded onto the truck outside woke Edith at five o'clock that morning. This meant that Father, the boys and Mary Ann were finished with the milking and would soon come in for breakfast.

Edith jumped out of bed into the frigid room. Her teeth chattered as she groped her way to the library table across the room. She ran her fingers over the top of the table and found the matches. She removed one from the container and struck it across the bottom of the library table. The match sparked as the flame caught. Her cold hand almost knocked the kerosene lamp over. She removed the globe and held the match over the wick until it caught. She replaced the globe and turned the flame down, so its brightness would not wake her younger sister, Emma.

Edith's breath was frosty in the cold air as she hurried into her heavy black stockings. She removed her flannel nightgown. She shivered as she pulled on her cold dress, which had been in the freezing room overnight.

She hurried from the cold room, and down the dark steps. She opened the kitchen door slowly, allowing her eyes to adjust to the brightness of the kitchen lamp, which hung above the table on a silver chain and illumined the center of the kitchen.

"Mother, Lydia, the lamp is smoking," she cried as she noticed smoke blackening the mantle.

"Hush, you'll wake the baby. Lydia, turn the lamp lower," said Mother all in one breath without turning her face away from the stove.

Lydia turned the little knob that lowered the flame. She did everything gracefully and easily. Edith wanted to be grown-up just like Lydia, but she was only a six-year-old girl.

On top of the black stove, Mother had two large skillets. They were sizzling hot and grease was splattering from them over the clean stove and over Mother's hands and arms as she turned the food with a spatula. Mother's prayer covering strings had become untied and she appeared agitated.

Edith sniffed the air. The kitchen was filled with the odor of hot grease and burning mush. "Oh, Mother, are we having mush?" Edith asked. She was so tired of home fried potatoes. The family ate them every morning all through the summer months. But now she smelled mush. "And gravy too?" she asked before Mother had time to reply to her first question. Edith was just as tired of puddings on top of her potatoes.

"No," Mother replied shortly. Her face was red from the grease and her arms had tiny blister spots from the grease.

Before Edith had time to pout, Mother said, "Go wash your hands, and don't make a fuss." Lydia took the dipper and scooped hot water from the basin without being asked. Edith added a little water from the cold-water bucket until the water was just right. A minute later Mary Ann came in from the barn. She washed with the same water that Edith had used.

When Father and the older boys came into the house, the peculiar smell of cows invaded the kitchen with them. It blended with the odor of hot grease and created the scent that announced the beginning of a Lancaster County farm day.

While Harvey was washing his hands, he whispered to Raymond, "The front cow is going to have a calf."

"I don't believe you. You think you know everything."

"I do. Just wait and see," Harvey was thirteen, and he never let eleven-year-old Raymond forget that he (Harvey) was two years smarter.

"What are you two boys whispering about?" asked Father.

"Ah, nothing," answered the boys in unison with innocent faces.

A stumping from the stairs and the banging of doors announced the appearance of nine-year-old John and eight-year-old Floyd.

"Be quiet," Mother admonished. "You'll wake the baby." Baby Alice was only a few months old, but the household schedule was altered to suit her needs. She wanted milk every four hours, she had to be held when she cried, and everybody had to be quiet when she slept.

Mother had been in bed the day the doctor had brought Alice, so Mary Ann and Lydia did all the work for ten days until Mother was well enough to get out of bed. They even held Baby Alice at night when she cried. Lots of visitors came to see the new baby. "We now have seven sons and seven daughters," Father told the visitors.

Father did not talk much about his first wife who had died of the 1918 flu. Then Edith's Mother had come to keep house for Father, and take care of his six small children. A year later they had gotten married. Now Father's two oldest daughters (Fannie and Edna) were married. Ivan was hired out and came home only on weekends. Mary Ann and Lydia helped at home. So did David Jr.

These six older children were Edith's half brothers and half sisters, but they looked whole, the same as the rest of the family.

As soon as Mother had breakfast prepared, Father opened the lids on top of the stove's firebox, and stamped down the wood with the poker. The wood broke into fiery red pieces. Then Father poured coal into the open top before he closed it with the round lid.

"The fire feels good this morning. It is cold outside. I guess it is time to start stripping tobacco," Father said. They always stripped tobacco in winter. But now they were all hungry.

They bowed their heads in a silent prayer before they ate. They were nearly finished eating before five-year-old Henry and two-year-old Emma appeared.

"Come here, Emma," Mother said, and she lifted her into the high chair. Father seated Henry on the bench behind the table, and gave him a piece of homemade bread spread with apple butter; 'the staff of life' he called it.

As soon as breakfast was over, John and Floyd grabbed their coats and hats and ran outside. Edith ran for her coat but Lydia saw her.

"You stay here and help me with the dishes," she said. Edith was afraid to disobey Lydia with Mother right there, but she stuck her tongue out at her behind Mother's back. Lydia only smiled.

When the dishes were done, Edith grabbed her coat and cap and ran outside. She wanted to get away before Lydia thought of something else that had to be done.

Everyone was in the cow stable, so Edith trailed in too. A tiny wet calf with wobbly legs was trying to suck milk from the teats of the cow that stood in the front stall. David was holding the calf's head against the cow's udder until the tiny mouth found the teat. Milk ran from its mouth as it drank. Harvey was trying to catch Raymond's eye. Raymond ignored him, but Edith was curious. Where did that calf come from? She had asked Lydia once, but Lydia had only said she was too young to know about such things.

Soon Father looked at his watch. "Harvey, it is time for you children to get ready for school," he announced.

"Come on, children," ordered Harvey. The five scholars trooped into the house. The four boys had to wash their hands and faces only. Edith had to have her long hair combed. Because she was so gentle Lydia combed slowly. When Mother combed she combed much faster, but it hurt more.

"Hurry up, Lydia. The boys will go without me," scolded Edith.

"I think I'll make only one braid today," Lydia teased. But Edith knew Lydia would braid her hair in two long braids and tie up the ends as usual.

Now, Mother was holding Baby Alice. As soon as Lydia had finished her last braid, Edith grabbed her lunch box. She paused beside Mother, and gently touched Alice's soft pink toe, then she hurried after her brothers.

Chapter 2

Spring

The winter of 1935 was almost over. The last snow was melting, causing little rivulets to gather beside the road. Early birds were returning to the Pennsylvania farmlands extending hope for an early spring.

Father had sold last year's tobacco crop. Some of the money he had put in the bank to use during the summer months, when there would not be enough income to cover his need. Some he used to pay his debts.

"Will you buy us a new wagon to play with now?" Edith asked, hopefully.

"I don't believe we will have any money left, after we have bought everything we need," Father teased.

Edith knew he was half serious, because the whole family needed new clothes. Father's trousers were in terrible shape. Mother had mended patch upon patch on his everyday ones. There was almost more patch than trousers; Mother had declared.

One day Father hitched old Dewey to the carriage and took Mother to New Holland, where they bought a great supply of ready-made shirts for the boys, lots of material for dresses for the girls and fabric for father's trousers.

While they were at the store, Edith and Henry were playing near the driveway and waiting for their parents to come home. As soon as they saw Dewey turn into the driveway they ran toward the carriage.

"Is there any money left for toys?" they hollered, before Father had stopped Dewey.

"Hush, the whole neighborhood will hear you," Mother warned, but she gave Father an amused glance.

"Well, now," Father drawled slowly with a twinkle in his eyes, "we needed an awful lot of things. It took most of our money, but—"

Edith and Henry waited, breathlessly. "But," Father continued, "we did get a lot of green stamps."

"Oh." Then Mother explained that they had gotten enough green stamps with their purchases, to get a tricycle for them.

"We will play mailman. I will ride and you will give me the mail," Henry told Edith later.

"No, I am the oldest. I get the first ride," argued Edith.

"I am the youngest! I get the first ride," contradicted Henry.

One day, Mother finally came home with that tricycle. It was green and bright and shiny. The children spent many happy hours delivering mail, but Edith could never remember who got the first ride.

Along with spring, came warmer and longer days. This put new life into the hens. They began laying more and larger eggs. Mary Ann was hired out, now that Alice was older, so Lydia and Mother cleaned all those eggs by themselves. They used a wet rag. If they were not careful, they squeezed the eggs too hard. Then the shell would break and the slippery insides would slide through their fingers, messing up the kitchen floor. Mother would grade the eggs by their feel in her hands. There were small, medium and large ones.

Every Thursday, Father delivered the eggs to the General Store in Hinkletown. There he would exchange them for groceries. Usually, the money for the eggs did not cover the grocery bill for Father's large family. Sometimes George Fair, the owner of the store, assembled the groceries while Father did other errands.

One day, Mother went along to the store. They handed George the store bill, as usual, and left to do other errands. When they returned, a very puzzled George handed the store bill back to Mother. "What does this mean?" he asked.

Across the bottom of the bill, Lydia, who thought only Mother would see the store bill, had written, 'my man needs a new pair of pants.' Mother was embarrassed but it was true. Father needed a new pair of trousers, but Lydia needed a new Sunday apron even more. She had been invited to a wedding to be a table waiter. She had absolutely nothing to wear.

So Mother helped her lay her pattern on the scant material they had. Mother laid and re-laid that pattern until she got it to fit on the material, so that Lydia could cut it out and sew her apron.

"I don't believe I could lay that pattern on the material in any other way to make it fit," declared Mother. On the floor, lay a small patch of that pretty material. Edith picked it up, and cut it in two pieces.

"Edith, what are you doing?" Lydia was horrified. "That is my apron pocket."

"It was on the floor," Edith sobbed. Mother could not find a piece big enough for another pocket. Lydia had to sew a seam right through the middle of that pocket.

Edith was so sorry that she did not go near the sewing machine when Mother started on Father's trousers. She watched from the other end of the room. When Mother turned the wheel on top of the machine, it started the treadle underneath the machine. Then Mother's feet took up the rhythms of the treadle on top of the machine. Her fingers moved the material, as she skillfully helped it through the machine's needle.

Grown-ups did things so easily. Edith wondered how it felt to be a grown-up, and be able to do everything so smoothly.

As Mother sewed she talked. "It is almost time for Elam Kreider to come. He usually comes in April."

Sure enough, a few days later Kreider's Model T Ford came chugging down the road and turned into the Fox driveway.

"Mother! Lydia! Kreider is here," Edith was filled with anticipation, for Kreider gave each child a whole stick of chewing gum. Kreider was a traveling salesman. When he first came to the Foxes he drove a white horse, but now he had the old Ford. He walked with the aid of a cane because his legs were crippled. Since he was so far from home, he stayed overnight and ate breakfast with the family. Then he would continue on his route.

Today Father carried Kreider's two black suitcases into the house after supper. As soon as Kreider opened them, Edith and the other young children crowded in front of the grown-ups until Mother told them to move back.

Everything in those cases was so fascinating. There were bottles upon bottles of flavorings and medicines. Mother bought enough things to last until Kreider's next visit. Then Kreider reached into his coat pocket and took out two packs of chewing gum and gave everyone, except Father and Mother, a piece of gum. Edith's piece smelled so good, she stuck it into her mouth right away. She forgot to remove it that night. When she woke up the next morning her jaws ached. She had been chewing all night.

The day after Kreider left, the steam engine came to steam Father's tobacco beds. The engine was there in the morning when Edith woke up. It had come sometime during the night and had gotten Father out of bed. It made an awful racket. There were two wheels at the back of the engine, and two smaller ones in the front; one on each side. A metal roof covered the steering wheel and the engine. A cart was fastened to the back of the engine. It held two large rectangular trays, which the men turned upside down on the tobacco bed. The trays were attached to the engine with a hose. Hot steam blew into the ground through the hose and killed the weed seeds. Father and the steam engine driver moved the trays every fifteen minutes. A shrill whistle reminded Father when it was time to move the trays. Edith and Floyd watched the steam rise when the trays were lifted.

"Let's get some eggs," Floyd shouted as he raced toward the hen house. So he and Edith each put an egg under the steam engine tray. When the men lifted the trays, the eggs were hard-boiled. Floyd ate two, but Edith ate only one. She did not like the groundy taste.

As soon as the steaming was finished, the steam driver drove the engine to the next farm. Father said that during the steaming season the steam engine never stopped. It only rested on Saturday at twelve midnight for Sunday, and started up on Sunday after midnight when another driver took over and moved the engine from farm to farm.

Now that the steaming was done for the year, Father had to get his tobacco seeds ready for sowing. Edith watched as he dropped four tablespoons of seeds into each two-quart glass jar.

"You better watch out or I'll get your nose in the jar," Father teased. Edith drew back a little. Father sprinkled just enough water into each jar to moisten the seeds until they clung to the sides of the jars. Everyday he would moisten the seeds. When black seeds turned white, it meant they had sprouted and were ready to sow into the tobacco beds.

When watching Father with the black seeds, Edith remembered that Lydia had put tobacco seeds into the pepper shakers by mistake one day.

"How did they taste?" she asked Father now.

"What?" Father asked.

"The seeds. How did they taste?"

"Oh," Father laughed, "I don't remember, but I hope Lydia remembers where the pepper is now."

"It was not my fault," Lydia answered. "Mother did not tell me that she put the tobacco seeds in the cupboard near the pepper."

"I thought it was strange that I could not taste that pepper and that nobody sneezed," laughed Father.

"I guess the cats were glad that it happened. They got a whole plate of mashed potatoes," Edith remembered.

Soon the seeds that Father had put into the jars were ready to sow in the tobacco beds. Father filled the watering can with water. Then he added the sprouted seeds. As he watered, the seeds sprayed from the watering can into the tobacco beds. Then Father covered the beds with a thin muslin sheet to shield the fine seeds from a lingering frost and from the hot noonday sun. As the plants grew bigger, they were pulled out of the beds and planted into the fields.

As soon as Father had time he prepared the garden for Mother. He plowed and raked the ground until it was almost as fine and soft as the tobacco beds were. Then he took the hoe and scratched rows, and Mother sowed lettuce, sugar peas and shell peas. She also planted small onions. Later, when the weather turned warmer and milder she sowed other seeds. While Father helped Mother, the older boys prepared the fields for Father's crops of corn, tobacco, wheat and hay.

When Mother was finished with the garden, she and Lydia started with the semi-annual house cleaning. The attic was done first. Lydia brushed all the cobwebs from the ceiling and the walls. Then she and Mother moved all the old furniture that was stored there, and the empty boxes, so they could sweep underneath. They scrubbed the floor with hot water and soap. When they had washed the windows and finished the floor, they hung neatly washed and ironed curtains at the windows. It took them only half a day to finish the attic.

The rooms that were used as bedrooms were much harder to clean. Directly after breakfast the men moved the heavy furniture into another room. Then Mother and Lydia moved the light furniture. They took the straw ticking off the bed and threw it out of the window. "Edith, get the scissors and take the ticking into the barnyard. Cut it open and remove the old straw," demanded Mother. "Then take the clean ticking and fill it with clean straw."

"Ah, Mother," complained Edith, "I don't like new straw. It doesn't have a hole to nestle in."

"You can make one tonight when you go to bed," Mother suggested. "Now get to work and don't argue." So Edith filled the ticking with stiff new straw, while Lydia and Mother swept, washed and scrubbed the floor of the bedroom.

After the noon meal, the men took the four pieces of rag carpet, one at a time and shook and shook them, until no more dust flew off.

Then Mother and Lydia laid down the carpet on the floor. The men put back the heavy furniture, then returned to their work in the fields. It took the women the rest of the afternoon to put everything back into place. It took them two weeks to clean the whole house.

Edith hated house cleaning. Everything was in disorder, and if Edith stayed to watch Mother and Lydia clean, they put her to work. To escape work she hid behind the barn. When she got there Floyd was there too. Together they swung in the apple tree branches and played in the dust beneath the plum tree. When they added water they could make pretty things. One day John had shown her how to make a beautiful mud hen. The mud hen was sitting on a mud nest. In the nest under her were eight little mud eggs.

When Edith came into the house that day, Mother scolded her, "You are all dirty, go wash your hands and face at once, and put on a clean dress."

Edith thought playing in the mud was so much fun. She decided if she ever had a little girl, she would never scold her for playing in the mud.

Chapter 3

The Young Children

The sun was hot in the sky and it beat down mercilessly. Edith was sitting on the seat of the topless buggy. The buggy stood in the shade of a small tree in Martindale. Sunshine filtered through the tree leaves and on Edith.

Old Dewey was hitched to the buggy and tied to the tree. Edith was watching a fly that had alighted on Dewey's rump. Dewey swished his tail, but the fly was too near to the beginning of Dewey's tail to get the full impact of his tail swish. It did not move. Dewey twitched his skin and stamped his foot, all to no avail. The movement of his body released a sweaty, horsy smell that Edith hardly noticed as she had her eyes on the fly. At last, she cautiously climbed from the buggy and stood behind Dewey.

"I am not going to hurt you," she told him. "I just want to get rid of that ugly fly." Then she slapped him directly where that fly had been, only it wasn't there anymore. "I missed it," she told Dewey. "But it flew away, so it won't hurt you again." As Edith climbed back into the buggy, she noticed that little celluloid squirrel again. Only a few minutes before Edith and Mother had gone into the store at Martindale. In the store was a basket filled with toy animals. Each animal was sitting on a tiny perch. Edith gazed longingly at those animals.

"Come on Edith. We don't have money for such things," said Mother. But the storekeeper had seen Edith's longing gaze. He picked up a squirrel that had become unglued from its perch.

"Would you like this one?" he asked Edith. Edith looked inquiringly at Mother. Mother nodded her head, and Edith's eyes began to sparkle as she nodded her head to the storekeeper. The squirrel did not cost one penny, because it had become loose from its perch.

"What do you say?" reminded Mother.

"Thank you," said Edith shyly, as she took that beautiful treasure. Now, sitting in the buggy with that beautiful squirrel, she fondled it softly and admired its wonderful soft tan color.

Now Mother was somewhere in that big building across the street. This was the second time she had entered that building in a very short time, while Edith had to wait in the buggy.

"Why can't I go along inside?" she had questioned.

"You just can't," Mother had answered. "Now play with your nice squirrel."

Mother had brought the big fourteen-quart kettle along from home. She had taken it into the big building.

While Edith waited a bee buzzed by. It flew to a flower and alighted there. Suddenly a hummingbird appeared and hovered over the same flower, and then it flew to a nearer flower. Edith held her breath hoping the hummingbird would

stay, but Dewey stamped his foot and the hummingbird flew away.

All of a sudden Edith realized she was hot. She pushed her long sleeves back and removed her sunbonnet and used it for a fan. When she wiggled her toe, a fly that had settled there flew away, but she hardly noticed it. She was watching the door of the big building. Suddenly it opened and Mother appeared. Her black bonnet covered her head and ears. Its two ribbons were tied under her chin. Her dress was dark and ample, but it was neatly fitted and carefully sewed. On her feet were black stockings and black shoes. In her hand was the big kettle all wrapped in newspapers? As soon as Mother reached the buggy, she set the kettle in front of Edith on the buggy floor.

"What is in the kettle and why is it wrapped?" Edith wanted to know. Mother pretended she didn't hear. She untied Dewey.

"Back, Dewey, back," she urged him until he was back far enough that she could turn him around. She held the lines as she climbed into the buggy. Then she slapped the lines over Dewey's back until he broke into a trot.

"Why is the kettle wrapped, Mother?" she repeated. This time Mother answered.

"You will have to wait and see."

"Ah, Mother." Edith wished she were a grown-up so she could act mysterious like Mother. Mother had been a little girl once. Edith did not know how she became a grown-up.

While Edith was musing her bare feet were dangling. They came against the paper wrapped kettle. It was ice cold.

"Ice cream! Oh Mother! Ice cream!" she shouted joyously.

"Hush, people will hear you," Mother admonished, for they were passing a row of houses. Mother kept urging Dewey to a trot. Edith knew Mother was afraid the ice cream would melt. Dewey was hot and he wanted to walk, but at last they were home.

Although it was the middle of the afternoon, everybody stopped work to eat ice cream. There were two delicious flavors. First Edith tasted the banana-flavored kind, letting it melt on her tongue. Then she tried the vanilla flavor. She ate and ate until she could eat no more. She was glad ice cream melted, so they could eat it all at once.

After they were finished eating, Mother glued Edith's squirrel back on its perch. Lydia hung it at the entrance, above the parlor door.

"Who wants a dead squirrel hanging around?" Henry taunted, so Edith knew he wanted one too.

One day Edith and Emma were playing in the front room. This room was cooler than the rest of the house, which was the reason Lydia put two delicious cakes into that room on the table to cool. They had beautiful white frosting on them. One was a sponge cake with a hole in the middle. The other was a layer cake.

"Don't you dare touch them," Lydia had warned her sisters sternly. They did not dream of disobeying that tone of voice.

Soon little Alice entered the room, and spied those beautifully frosted cakes. She glanced at the sponge cake which had the hole in the center of the cake, then she glanced at the layer cake. She put her tiny fingers against the layer cake and dug a hole right in the center of the cake. Her little fist came up with a hunk of cake, which she stuffed into her mouth.

Edith and Emma stood there and stared, dumbfounded by Alice's daring deed. They could not move. They just stood there, rooted to the spot. Then Lydia entered the room.

Alice looked at Lydia's face and began to cry. "I wanted to make a hole in the other cake," she sobbed.

"Edith, why didn't you stop her? You knew better even

if she didn't," roared Lydia. Suddenly Edith's feet could move again. She took a running dive out the front door. Emma followed. Whatever had held them powerless abruptly released its hold on them, and Edith began to giggle. She giggled and giggled. Emma joined in. They giggled until they cried.

They did not dare set foot in the house until they sobered up. That took until suppertime. Lydia still looked cross but she didn't say a word.

One morning, not long after the cake incident, Edith felt sick. Her cheeks swelled up and she lost her appetite. She lay on the studio couch in the front room. John was sick too. Mother had pulled two chair seats together, put a soft comforter on the chairs, and made a bed for him there. Emma was not feeling well either. She lay on Mother's big bed in the other room. The doctor said they had the mumps. Floyd and Henry were recuperating and they were noisy. The noise made Edith's head throb. She just lay there hurting. Because Edith was always hungry for candy, Mother gave her some jelly beans to tempt her appetite, but she was too sick to eat them.

As soon as Mother left the room, Henry started begging, "May I have your candy?" When Father bought a pound of candy, and each child had a piece, the candy would be gone, so Henry was always hungry too.

"I will eat them when I feel better," Edith replied.

"But they will spoil by then," Henry replied. "May I have them now before they spoil?"

"Let me alone. I want to rest."

"May I have them, Edith, may I?" begged Henry.

Edith was too sick to listen to Henry's begging, so she got those jelly beans from the windowsill where Mother had placed them. She looked at Henry's expectant face. His eager eyes made her realize just how delicious those jelly beans were. She popped them into her mouth and became very sick. Many years passed before she could eat jelly beans again.

Chapter 4

Sunday

The sun neared the horizon in a realm of beautiful sunset glows, while Father searched the skies with a knowing gaze. He read the skies like Edith read a book.

"We will have beautiful weather tomorrow," he predicted. "The whole family can go to church."

So Mother laid the younger children's Sunday clothing neatly on a chair in their bedrooms on Saturday evening. She and Lydia bathed the youngest children, but Edith filled the hand basin with warm soapy water, and bathed all by herself in her bedroom. Mother only checked her ears.

Sunday morning dawned with a chill. Mother started the fire in the range with fine pieces of wood and corncobs thrown in disorderly fashion on the grate. She poured a small amount of kerosene on the kindling and lit it with a match. The kindling burst into a blazing fire. After the fire had burned down a bit, Mother added larger pieces of wood gradually, so she would not smother the flame.

"Get the frying pan, Lydia, and put the potatoes in to fry, while I wash the kerosene smell from my hands."

Built into the kitchen floor was a handle that Lydia pulled and a dumbwaiter glided up into the kitchen from the cool cellar. Inside its screened door were four shelves that were filled with food. Lydia removed the dish of thin sliced potatoes and placed them in the greased skillet to make home fries.

Nobody slept late on Sunday morning. Even Alice was up by the time the men had finished the outside chores. Before every meal the family bowed their heads in a silent grace. After the silent prayer Father asked Emma, "Do you want butter or just apple butter on your bread?"

Emma was sleepy and cross this morning. "I don't want bread." One look at Father's face changed her mind. "Just apple butter," she replied. Father wanted everyone to eat bread. He believed it was the staff of life, but he only gave Emma one-fourth of those big homemade bread slices, because she was so little. Henry's piece had a brown crust that he tore off. When Father's attention was diverted he slipped it between the framework of the table. Edith was tired of homemade bread and apple butter too, so she stuffed her bread into her mouth, chewed it slightly and swallowed it in one big lump. She liked the potatoes and gravy better. This morning they even had corn flakes and shredded wheat. Because this was Sunday, it took too long to cook oatmeal when they were getting ready to go to church.

Mary Ann was home today. She came home over the weekend. She helped Lydia wash the dishes, while Mother washed the children's hands and faces. After all the morning tasks were finished, Father asked, "Can you be ready to leave as soon as I have Dewey hitched up?"

"I think we can be ready, if you take Emma along out with you." So Father put Emma's covering on her head and tied it under her chin. Next came her bonnet. Then he slipped on her coat, took hold of her hand and led her to the carriage. After he had lifted her into the carriage, he went to the barn to fetch Dewey. When Mother and Lydia were ready they sat in the back seat. Because the seat was so narrow Mother held Alice in her lap and Lydia held Emma. Then Father drew up the folded-down front seat for himself and Edith and Henry to sit on.

Floyd, John, Raymond and Harvey rode their bicycles, while David and Mary Ann used the top buggy. Although they were early this morning, John Brubaker (neighbor) drove past while Father was helping Henry and Edith into the carriage.

"I wish I could be ready before he is, just one time," sighed Father.

"You have plenty of time. It is not quite seven thirty," replied Mother.

As they drove along Edith wondered, "Why do people with cars sit on the other side of the seat?"

"Because their steering wheel is on that side," Father teased, then he became serious. "Before there were paved roads, there were deep ditches and mud holes by the side of the road. So you had to sit on this side to see those holes. You wouldn't want that to happen, would you?"

Top Buggy
The Lancaster County Old Order Mennonites no longer use the top buggy. The young folks now drive the one-seat carriage.

"I hope John Brubaker will get stuck, so we can get there first," Edith decided.

The Fox family arrived at church in plenty of time as Mother had predicted. Dewey would not stand still long enough for the family to climb out of the carriage, so father drove him to the hitching post and tied him, so everyone could get out.

Mother and the girls entered the church building through an anteroom that had hundreds of clothing hooks along the walls and on racks in the middle of the room. Mother and her friends hung their dark shawls and black bonnets at the end of the room. Lydia and her friends grouped together at the further end of the room to remove their dark wraps.

In the middle of the room, Edith and the younger girls gathered. They removed brightly colored bonnets and cheerfully hued coats. Because they did not belong to the church yet, they did not dress so strictly.

The mothers with very small children walked into the main room and sat down as soon as they had removed their wraps, but the young girls waited for their friends to arrive, then they entered the main room in a long single file line and sat on their respective benches.

Father waited outside until Dewey had cooled enough to have his blanket thrown over his back and pinned down. There was no room in the church for the men's coats, so Father removed his overcoat and laid it on the carriage seat. Then he hurried into the warm church building, from the men's side, directly into the main room. Above the men's heads was a ceiling rack. Here Father hung his big black hat.

The boys entered the building noisily, their shoes thumping on the wooden floor as they walked in a long single file row and sat on their seats. Soon the church was crowded. Rows of chairs were set beside the benches, but some of the women with babies stayed in the anteroom. The room buzzed with whispering and gossiping as friend greeted friend. Finally nine o'clock arrived, and a song leader announced the number of a page in the hymnbook. All whispering ceased and the German hymn began with notes sung from memory.

Meanwhile, the bishop, preachers and deacons (all men) were in a small room of their own. A few minutes after the first hymn began, the door to this room opened and the clergy entered the main room. They sat on a bench against the wall. In front of them was a small table, which held a Bible and served as a pulpit. In front of the pulpit was a long narrow table. Here sat the song leaders, which also included only men. As soon as the first verse was sung, the leaders waited for the clergy to suggest another hymn or to continue with the original one.

To the right of the clergy were rows of long benches, one in back of the other, that were filled with wives. On the right of the wives sat the young and the unmarried girls. To the clergy's left sat the husbands, and to their left were the young boys and the unmarried men.

After two hymns were sung, one of the preachers stood up. Edith loved to listen to this particular preacher. He had a pleasant singsong voice and he always began his sermon with the same words.

"*Free-da sein in dee-sem house*," meaning, Peace be to this house. Then he went on to explain how Christ said those words when He entered a house. The whole sermon was in High German. (This is not the Pennsylvania German that is generally spoken in Lancaster County.) Although Edith knew the meaning of most of those big German words, a few still puzzled her.

The beginning sermon was about one-half hour long, then the preacher said, "Now if you are one and at peace with me, let us kneel in a silent prayer." After the prayer the congregation resumed their seats. Then the deacon stood and read a portion of the scripture, again in German, to be used as the text for the next preacher.

The second and next preacher spoke on every verse of the text. Most Mennonite preachers are harsh and penetrating in rephrasing the Gospel according to their particular faith, and this preacher was no exception.

Edith's thoughts wandered. She wished she could sit on a bench further back with the girls her own age, but she must sit with Emma because she was such a crybaby. Emma was too big to sit with Mother, and Edith thought she was too big to sit with Emma. Besides these straight wooden benches were hard and they had no backs. The benches for the girls her own age, had backs. So Edith wiggled and squirmed until Mother gave her a sharp look. Then Edith settled down, outwardly.

At last the preacher ended his sermon and sat down. Then Edith ceased her daydreaming, she knew the sermon would soon be over. While seated, all the preachers and the deacons, each spoke a few minutes, agreeing with the main preacher's sermon. Then the preacher rose again declaring his accordance before asking the audience to kneel for an audible prayer. After the prayer the congregation stood and remained standing as the benediction was pronounced. Then they sat for the final hymn. The two and one-half hour sermon was over at last. There would not be another service at Martindale for four whole weeks.

Two other Mennonite groups shared this building on the Sundays that the Old Order Mennonites had meetings in other church buildings. When the last hymn was sung, everybody stood up. Some people pushed and shoved to get out of the building in a hurry, but others stood and visited blocking the entrance. Empty folding chairs stood in the aisles adding to the chaos.

Sometimes Father and Mother invited company to their home for dinner, but today they had not prepared for visitors.

It was after one o'clock when the family arrived home.

While Father and the boys watered and fed the animals, Mother started the fire in the range, and prepared tomato soup. The girls set the table and washed the dishes. In the afternoon, the younger children played, while the parents and the older children rested and read the Bible. The Old Order Mennonites do not take their Bibles along to church. They read the text at home.

Mother sometimes played table games with the children, but tonight the family went to bed early. They had refreshed their souls, now they would refresh their bodies.

Old Order Mennonites—Uncle Harry Fox and Aunt Lizzie Fox. Aunt Lizzie had her back turned while closing the shed door. Martha was ready with her camera when she said, "Lizzie," Aunt Lizzie turned and Martha snapped the picture. Uncle Harry, who had been watching, was surprised when he was on the picture too.

Chapter 5

A Rainy Day

The birds were singing. The trees were in full summer dress. On the farm there was no end to the work that needed to be done. But the strangest thing was happening on this busy summer day. Father and Mother dropped their work and decided to go for a walk up the lane. This was in the middle of the week. It was strange and mysterious, but Edith was happy. She always enjoyed a walk with the family.

Then Father said, "Edith, you stay here with Lydia." This added to the strangeness that was puzzling Edith. Not even one of the children was allowed to go with their parents on that walk.

Edith sat on the settee, pondering this strange turn of events. "I can't understand it," she told Lydia. "We always go along when they go for a walk. It is strange."

"Maybe they will have a baby in the morning," tantalized Lydia.

"I bet that is it," replied Edith, who needed something to believe. Besides she vaguely remembered how strange Mother had acted before Alice was born. She hid in the house when a stranger came to the door and she did other strange things too.

Early next morning Edith awoke. She needed no urging to get up. She jumped out of bed, dressed in the dark, and ran down the familiar steps, into the brightly lit kitchen. She looked all around for the new baby.

Lydia was setting the table, and Mother was working at the stove. There was no new baby anywhere. Everything was strangely familiar. Edith ran outside and hid in the woodshed that was beside the outhouse. She needed time alone to hide her bewilderment.

She now knew that Lydia had tricked her again. If only she were a grown-up, nobody could trick her. She would know everything.

When the rains began a few days later, she forgot all about that strange day. She pressed her face against the window and it was still raining. It was just too much for Edith. "Why doesn't it stop raining? I hate rain!" she complained.

"Edith!" Father was shocked. "Aren't you ashamed of yourself? Complaining about rain! Just think what would happen if the good Lord would not send rain. Nothing would grow, and everyone would starve."

When Edith hung her head, repentantly, Father spoke in a softer tone, trying to cheer her. "What do you think the people in Germany do when it rains?" he teased.

"They let it rain," she answered. Then she added, "Did your grandfather tell you that?" and Father smiled.

Edith's great-grandfather had come from the old country, and she never tired of hearing the story.

"Tell me about my great-grandfather," she pleaded. So Father settled down in the big creaky rocker, with Alice on his one knee and Emma on the other knee. Henry sat on the floor, but Edith sat on the high-backed chair, because she was a girl. Edith hated being a girl, because there were so many things a girl must not do. She must not jump, so her dress would not float above her knees. She must always sit with her dress modestly below her knees. But sometimes she jumped and played rough games with her brothers when her parents could not see her. However today she behaved.

Soon Father began his story, "Your great-grandfather was born in Hessa Darmstadt, Germany. At that time a new law in Germany required everyone to have military training. Your great-grandfather did not want to learn to kill. He believed in loving everyone."

As Father was speaking, Edith was watching a fly crawl around the side of his head. Father's skin was tough from years of outdoor work. He did not feel the fly as it journeyed toward his baldhead.

When Father would come into the house after working in the field, he always washed his head. It got as dirty as his hands and face. Although Father's skin was tough, his baldhead was tender.

This fly was headed toward that tender spot. Edith nudged Henry until he noticed the fly too. Together they watched the fly crawl along. Suddenly, Father shook his head, and the fly took a short spin. Then it dropped right back onto Father's head. Edith and Henry had to laugh when Father took a slap at that pest and missed, but the fly stayed away and Father resumed his story.

"When your great-grandfather was eighteen, he escaped from Germany by becoming a stowaway on board a ship bound for America. He had no money to pay for his stolen passage, so he worked on the ship to earn his way. The ship landed in Delaware, but the mosquitoes were so bad your great-grandfather stayed on board until the ship arrived in Maryland. Shortly thereafter a wind blew his hat away. What did he do then?" asked Father.

"He took a hat from a scarecrow, because he had no money to buy one," answered Edith who knew the story by heart.

"That is right. He had no money to buy a hat. Everything he owned was tied in his red handkerchief that he carried with him. As he walked by the side of the road, he stopped at farm houses and asked for work, but no one would hire a stranger. At last, he was in Lancaster County, Pennsylvania, near Amsterdam where he tried one more time to find work on a farm. The farm he stopped at was in a lane and was owned by an Amish man. But Christian Miller, the Amish man, did not trust this strange man with the foreign accent either.

"As your great-grandfather walked back out of the lane, he was very discouraged. He had followed the Good Lord, even to coming to this strange land. He felt deserted, having no job, no friends and no money.

"His despair was noted by Miller. Miller's conscience bothered him, so he sent his small son after your great-grandfather to tell him to come back, he would give him work.

"Now most of his troubles were over, because he was a good worker, but he was still a fugitive from Germany. He was afraid that if Germany would discover his whereabouts, they would take him back to his homeland. For this reason, he never went back to visit his parents. He never sent a letter directly to them, for fear their mail would be opened by the authorities.

"He died when I was sixteen," concluded Father. "Now I wish so much that I had asked him more about his life in Germany, while he was still with us."

Edith sighed. "I am glad I can stay right here at home. It must be awful never to see your family and friends again," she mourned.

Then she happened to glance out of the window, and she forgot all about her great-grandfather. "It stopped raining, and the sun is shining," she hollered joyously. She grabbed her sunbonnet and ran outside, slamming doors as she went, with Henry close at her heels.

They had been playing only a short time when the sun disappeared, and the rain came again.

"Are you going back inside?" asked Henry.

"No, I will have to work if I do."

"You won't have to work today, Mother was sewing patches."

"Are you sure?" asked Edith, for this meant Mother had extra time. She only worked at patches when the other work was finished.

"I saw her with my own eyes," declared Henry. "We can play with the table games if we go in."

"All right. I was getting wet anyway," agreed Edith.

As soon as Edith opened the kitchen door, Mother said, "Oh, there you are, Edith. I want you to set the table for supper." And she went about preparing the meal.

Items found in an old time kitchen.

"I thought you said she was sewing patches," Edith demanded, crossly, aside to Henry.

"She usually does when it rains. I must have gotten mixed up with some other time," replied Henry.

"You lied to me, now you should help set the table."

"That is girl's work," said Henry, haughtily.

And so were the dishes after supper, but Mother told Henry to fill the wood box. It was strange, how much better Edith felt after Henry had to do some chores too.

They did play table games later that evening, however it was soon bedtime. At least everyone thought it was bedtime, except Edith. She was in no mood for bed. She had played table games with everyone who would play, but she wanted to play some more.

"It is time for bed," said Father. "It is eight o'clock already."

Suddenly, the tears came. "I want to play a game of checkers," sobbed Edith, who actually wanted to play Parcheesi, but she knew Father never played Parcheesi.

"If you stop crying, I will play one game with you." Edith dried her tears and got out the checkerboard. Sometimes, she won the game when she played with Father, but tonight she lost the game and her tears started afresh.

"I want to play one more game," she sobbed.

"That is enough! You are tired. You are going to bed," Father said.

In bed, Edith's sobs kept time to the raindrops falling on the tin porch roof beside the bedroom window. Soon her sobs quieted as she fell asleep, but the rain continued.

Chapter 6

Money Activities

Lydia poured a dipper full of hot water into the dishpan. Then she dipped the ladle into the stove's reservoir (or tank) for more hot water. As she walked back and forth between stove and sink, the white strings that were attached to her prayer covering, floated behind her head.

"Don't just stand there and stare. Do something, Edith. Fill the reservoir with water. We will need more hot water later," she said.

Lydia began washing dishes at the dry sink. She was singing. Edith picked up the bucket and carried it to the back porch where the rainwater pump was. She filled the bucket, carried it inside and poured the water into the stove's tank. Soon the tank was filled. Lydia was still washing dishes and singing, "Rock Of Ages."

"Don't you ever get tired of working?" Edith wondered out loud.

"The work has to be done, so I might as well enjoy myself while doing it."

"I wish I was a grown-up," said Edith, wistfully.

"But then you would have to work," Lydia reminded her.

"Then, I would like to work," replied Edith, shrewdly.

"I'll tell you what. Practice working now, so you will learn to like it by the time you are a big girl. Fetch some drinking water too."

"Ah, Lydia, you tricked me," demurred Edith, but she picked up the well water bucket and headed for the pump house. The pump house for the drinking water stood in the front yard near the front gate. The whole neighborhood fetched their drinking water from this pump. They fetched water in their containers everyday for nineteen years, eleven months and twenty-nine days. Then for one whole day they were not allowed to fetch any water. This was strictly enforced by the government and by Edith's parents, so nobody would have a permanent right to the delicious well water.

That twenty-year day was strangely silent, as nobody came to speak a pleasant word. Edith was glad when that day was over. She liked to have the neighbors come over for that cool refreshing water. Sometimes they even brought their children along to play with the Fox children, while the parents visited for a few minutes.

Sometimes, Father asked Edith to turn a small gadget on the cement floor in the pump house. This caused the water to run through underground pipes to the cattle trough in the barnyard, when the handle was pumped. It took five hundred strokes of the pump handle to have enough water flow into the trough for all those thirsty cattle, sometimes even more. Edith's arms would ache from all that pumping. She was glad Father asked her to pump only when he was very busy. But today she only fetched one bucket of water for Lydia. Before Lydia could think of another job for her to do she ran outside.

As soon as the boys saw her, they called, "Hurry up, Edith, we must catch the baby pigeons today."

"Oh, boy, I am coming." Edith had forgotten this was Wednesday, the day for the huckster. The young pigeons must be caught at exactly the right stage of their growth. If they were too young, the huckster refused to take them. If they were too old, the children could not catch them.

Today there were five nests in the barn with squabs that were just the right size. Because she was a girl, she had to stay on the barn floor. Floyd was the oldest of the three, so he climbed the highest rafters. After he caught the young squabs, he handed them to Henry on the low rafters. Henry, in turn, handed them to Edith on the floor. She dropped them into the crate.

The young squabs had bulging eyes and under-developed feathers, but Edith loved to hold them anyway. Because the nests were hard to get at, it took the children a few hours, but when they were finished, they had ten squabs.

Henry and Floyd carried the crate out to the side of the road, while Edith trailed behind. The huckster would stop when he saw the crate. All he offered today was two dollars and fifty cents, for all ten squabs.

Floyd kept a whole dollar, because he was the oldest and he worked the hardest. Edith and Henry each received seventy-five cents. Edith was older than Henry, but Henry had climbed high and lifted heavier, so he was allowed to keep as much money as Edith did.

"It isn't fair," Edith grumbled. "I may not climb up on the rafters, even though I want to. But Henry gets just as much money, and he has the fun of climbing. It just isn't fair."

"You are lucky we share with you at all," answered Floyd. They put their pigeon money into the bank at New Holland. Edith already had put three whole dollars of pigeon money in the bank. Combined with her other money in the bank, she had almost twenty dollars in the bank. She would soon be rich.

Edith had never heard of an allowance but there were other ways of earning money. When Father had used all the tobacco plants he needed. The children planted the remaining plants in small plots in the apple orchard, between the trees. They hoed and picked weeds all summer. They also kept the worms off their plants.

The children helped Father hoe his plants for free, but when they picked tobacco worms from his plants, he paid them $0.05 for a thousand worms. It was not difficult to earn fifteen or twenty cents in half a day. In the fall, Father paid the children for their own tobacco. Edith's favorite way of earning money was the easiest of all. It was giving food to the neighbors.

"Edith, do you and Emma want to take some tomatoes (or corn or whatever they had) over to Will's place? We have more than we can use," Mother would say. Then Will's wife would ask the girls what their parents wanted for the tomatoes.

"They don't want anything. We have more than we can use, and Mother has canned all we can eat this winter."

"Well then, you keep this for yourself," and she would hand them a nickel, and sometimes a dime.

Edith's least favorite way of earning money was setting mouse traps. Every fall, as soon as it started getting colder outside, mice would somehow find an entry into the house. They tunneled through the walls and congregated in the cellar and the attic. There the children set traps for them.

Edith did not like to set traps. Sometimes her fingers slipped and she caught her fingers. Then she had to wait until her fingers stopped hurting, before she could reset the traps. For every mouse her trap caught, she received a whole penny that she did not need to share with anyone.

Edith did not always put her money in the bank. Sometimes she wanted things. She had been saving nickels and dimes all summer. She wanted a quarter, but nobody was going to the store. So she kept right on saving.

Then one day, Mother needed material. Father hitched up Dewey, and Edith and Mother left for New Holland. Mother was in a rare chummy mood. She did not seem like a grown-up at all. She seemed like Edith's friend. They talked of the weather, of their friends, and about happenings of the past. After a while Mother asked, "What are you going to buy with your money?"

"I am not sure. I want either colors or paints," replied Edith, who was an artist at heart. "I will know when I see them both."

"Do you know what they cost?" wondered Mother.

"They each cost twenty-five cents. I have forty-two cents," she added as an afterthought.

"I will give you eight cents, then you will have enough money to buy both," said Mother and she handed Edith eight shiny pennies.

"Just like that. Without having to do anything?" Edith could not believe her ears. She looked at Mother in surprise; but Mother only smiled and nodded her head.

Edith bought a box of sixteen beautiful crayons and a box of thirty-two brilliant watercolors. Every Sunday afternoon after church and on rainy days Edith took her coloring book, drew up a chair to the kitchen table, and colored or painted to her heart's content. She painted until her paints had water holes in them and her colors were broken into small pieces.

Chapter 7

School Days

The year was 1937, and it was a special one for Edith. She was going to enter the Secondary School at Hinkletown. She could hardly wait for the first day of school to begin. Now she could climb up that long flight of stairs to the upper room, and be a fifth grader.

Edith remembered the first day of school downstairs very well. The downstairs room had first, second, third and fourth grades. There was a lady teacher, who wore a short dress

Hinkletown School. Photo provided by Alice Rissler.

and had her hair cut. Mrs. Frankfort was old and Edith did not understand her at all. In fact, the problem had begun the first day of school, when Mrs. Frankfort had spoken to her in English.

Edith had been playing outside with Mary Brubaker, when Mrs. Frankfort appeared. She said something to Edith in English. Edith asked Mary, in Pennsylvania Dutch, what Mrs. Frankfort had said. Mary was Edith's neighbor and she was older. She had learned to speak English, but she was busy playing. She had her head turned when she answered. Edith did not understand her, so she repeated her question. Mary's head was still turned, and her answer was indistinct. Edith was ashamed to ask again, so she never did find out what Mrs. Frankfort had said.

Edith learned fast, however, so it did not take her long to learn the English language. But she always seemed to forget that when Mrs. Frankfort said, "First grade," she was speaking to Edith too. "Edith," Mrs. Frankfort would say then. "Edith," she repeated, louder. Suddenly, Edith would hear her name and see all the first grade students standing in front of the teacher's desk staring at her sitting at her desk.

Every morning, Edith and her brothers walked nearly a mile to school. Edith walked on the hard road surface during the summer, because it did not hurt her bare feet as the pebbles by the side of the road did. One evening as the children were walking home from school, Edith was walking on the road, heated by the sun. It warmed her bare feet, but her hands were still cold. She stuck them in her jacket pocket. Then she felt her mittens, pulled them out of her pocket, and put them on her hands.

When Mabel Horning, an older pupil, saw Edith she laughed and laughed. "Ho, ho, ho, mittens and no shoes. I never saw anything like it in my whole life. Ho, ho." Edith was so embarrassed; she never put on mittens again, unless she wore shoes.

Mrs. Frankfort had a drawer in her desk. In it she kept small pieces of candy. Sometimes she had sour balls. Sometimes there were jelly beans, but on this particular day it was candy corn. Mrs. Frankfort opened the drawer to remove something just as Edith was passing by. Edith pretended she did not notice, but her mouth watered so that she could hardly bear it. She saw that candy in her mind's eye, even after Mrs. Frankfort had closed the drawer. Edith thought of nothing else but that delicious candy during her lunch hour. As soon as Mrs. Frankfort had eaten her lunch, she closed her lunch box, and went out to the outhouse. One by one the other children finished their lunch and went out to play. Edith was alone in the schoolroom. She did not intend to take the candy. She only opened the drawer to look at it again. It looked so delicious. Edith's hand reached out and before Edith could stop them, her fingers grabbed a handful of that candy, and her feet ran outside. Her mouth found the candy as delicious as it looked.

Suddenly Edith felt guilty, but she had left some candy for Mrs. Frankfort, she reasoned. Perhaps she would not miss a few pieces, but Edith felt uncomfortable all afternoon.

Sometime during the afternoon, Mrs. Frankfort said, "I had some candy in my desk drawer. Someone took most of it. Now I am not going to mention any names, but I want you to know, that I know who that person is."

Edith knew Mrs. Frankfort did not suspect her, but she was shocked that a grown person would tell a lie. Although, she knew that stealing was wrong, she felt better, knowing Mrs. Frankfort had told a lie, which was wrong too.

Edith liked the huge black, barrel-shaped stove that stood up front near Mrs. Frankfort's desk. It kept the room warm and cozy during the cold, stormy winter days. The fourth grade boys carried the buckets of coal from the basement to feed that enormous stove. Mrs. Frankfort poured the coal into a door that opened at the front of the stove. Beneath it was a smaller door. This door was used to remove the burned coal that was now ashes. The bigger boys also carried them out.

Inside the top door was a shelf. It was just the right size to hold a few potatoes to bake for the students' lunch. Sometimes Edith brought a potato along to school. Then Mrs. Frankfort would take a pencil and print E.F. on it. She put everybody's potato on that stove shelf at the first recess. The potatoes would be soft by lunchtime, and were very delicious with salt and butter.

One morning when Edith went into the schoolroom, she was greeted by a sight that astonished her. Mrs. Frankfort had old gloves on her hands, and she was using a stove poker to get everything out of Lester Snyder's desk. Without touching anything with her hands, she carried everything that had been in that desk, including the new schoolbooks, to the stove and burned it.

Edith watched dumbfounded. "Why is she doing that?" she asked one of the pupils.

"Lester has scarlet fever, and it is very contagious," she

The schoolhouse photographed on June 10, 1938.

was told. Mrs. Frankfort scrubbed the inside and the outside of that desk, with brush and lye water. She scrubbed the floor all around the desk, and then she burned the gloves. No one else contracted that dreadful disease.

Now Mrs. Frankfort and the lower room were in the past. Now, Edith was in the upper room, and Mr. Wenger was her teacher. He taught fifth, sixth, seventh and eight grades.

Mr. Wenger made learning so much fun. Downstairs, Edith had not learned to recite the alphabet in rotation, nor did she know all of the multiplication table. It had been so dull to recite for Mrs. Frankfort, but now Edith did not want Mr. Wenger to think she was stupid, so she studied them both, industriously. She learned them both before Mr. Wenger found out how ignorant she had been.

Emma started first grade the same day Edith graduated to the upstairs room. One day someone knocked at the door. It was one of the lower grade students. Mrs. Frankfort wanted

*School friends. Left to right. Front row: Mary Beiler, **Edith Fox**, Anna Nolt, Mary Sensenig, and Esther Wenger. Back row: Betty Nolt, Annie Shirk, Mary Brubaker, Anna Belle Weaver, Edna Good, Susie Good, and Betty Leucy.*

Edith to come downstairs and sit with Emma, because she was crying. Henry was in the same room with Emma, but she just cried more when he came near. Edith did not want to sit with Emma. She did not want to be in the downstairs room again. But everyday Mrs. Frankfort had someone ask for Edith, and everyday Edith went downstairs and sat with Emma.

Then, one day when Mrs. Frankfort sent for Edith, Mr. Wenger said, "Edith, your sister has had enough time to adjust to school now. You stay here and let Mrs. Frankfort take care of Emma."

Edith was very grateful to Mr. Wenger, but she only said, "All right." She did not want him to know how much she

*1940-1941 Pupils. Left to right. First row: Unknown, Emanuel Beiler, Harold Horst, Mahlon Good, Verna Sensenig, Arlene Snyder, Unknown. Second row: Willa May Zoll, John Sensenig, Henry Fox, Ivan Weiler, Unknown, Aaron Horst, Eli Beiler. Third row: Unknown, Emma Weiler, Emma Nolt, Magadlena Good, Edna Hoover, Margaret Good, Harry Snyder, Emma Sensenig, Unknown. Fourth row: Rufus Hoover, Clayton Snyder, Eva Nolt Hilda Trego, Edna Martin, Betty Leicy, Anna Nolt, **Edith Fox**, Mr. (John) Wenger.*

hated to sit with Emma in the lower room, because Mother had said she was supposed to be kind to her sister.

Mr. Wenger sometimes assigned Edith's class to write stories. Edith loved to make up a story and read it to the whole class. She loved to have the other children and Mr. Wenger praise her stories.

One day the four girls and three boys in Edith's class had all written, and read their stories. The stories were all good, but Edith's was excellent.

"I want the class to vote for the person whom they believe has the best story," Mr. Wenger said. "If you think your story is the best, vote for yourself," he added. But Edith just could not do that. She could not vote for herself. It would be vain, and vanity was wrong. So she voted for a story that had been written by one of the boys. The three boys had all voted for Rufus, the boy that Edith had voted for. He had voted for himself too. The three girls had voted for Edith, but because she had not voted for herself, she had cast the deciding vote against her own story.

"Although, I will abide by your decision, I do not agree with it," Mr. Wenger told the class. This made Edith feel a little better.

Chapter 8

Growing Needs

dith heard Mary Ann and Lydia sneaking up the steps, but she pretended to be sound asleep. Sometimes she learned secrets that way.

Almost every Saturday night, David took Lydia and Mary Ann along to a singing in his new top buggy. They usually came home around midnight, then they would steal quietly up the steps, as they were doing tonight. They did not want to disturb Edith and Emma.

Now, Mary Ann was teasing Lydia. "I know someone asked you for a date. Come on, tell me who it was," she begged in a whisper.

Edith held her breath, but Lydia only answered, "You'll have to wait and see."

"Then, just tell me if you said, yes," begged Mary Ann.

Edith refrained from moving, but Lydia only said, "You'll have to wait and see."

"You are an old grouch," whispered Mary Ann, whose patience was running thin. "I always tell you when I have a date." Even that did not move Lydia to speak, so Edith drifted back to sleep.

The next day when Lydia came home from church, she helped Mother make dinner as usual. After dinner she went upstairs and slept awhile which was unusual.

That Sunday evening, just before seven o'clock, Lydia came downstairs wearing her Sunday dress and her good covering.

"Are you going somewhere?" wondered Edith aloud.

"Hush, you are too young to ask so many questions," admonished Mother. Just then, Edith spied a horse and buggy pulling into the Fox's driveway.

"Someone is coming," she cried happily, and opened the door to run out, and greet the visitor, but Mother's voice stopped her.

"Stay here. He is not coming to see us." Suddenly, Edith remembered last night's conversation, so she just watched from inside the house. The team drove under the shed roof. Soon a young man emerged from the buggy. He tied the horse and walked toward the gate.

Edith peeked out of the window and watched everything he did. He walked in the front yard, and up the set of porch steps that led to the outside parlor door. Now he was hidden from her view, but she heard a knock on the parlor door. Then it was being opened and a strange voice said, "Good evening."

"Good evening," replied Lydia's voice. Edith was surprised. How had Lydia slipped into the parlor and closed the door without her knowledge?

"You were so busy spying on that young man, you did not see Lydia go into the parlor," said Mother.

"Soon you will be growing up and starting to date too," observed Father. Edith wished he was right, but she just stayed little, no matter how hard she tried to grow up. Then Father turned to Mother. "They are all growing up so fast. It seems just like yesterday they were babies."

"Yes, they are growing, but the house is not growing with them," sighed Mother. "We need more room. We could build onto the summer kitchen."

The family had one kitchen where they spent their summers. It was built with only one wall touching the rest of the house, so it got all the cooling breezes. The winter kitchen had only one wall that was not enclosed by other rooms. It was warmer because the cold winds could not touch it.

"That would only help during the summer. You would still have a small winter kitchen," observed Father.

"We could stay in the summer kitchen all year. Now-a-days, many people do not move their kitchens with the seasons."

"It would get awful cold in the summer kitchen. It is facing the north, you know."

"We could put up another stove and the cooking range. We really do need the extra space," observed Mother.

"You got it all figured out, I see," said Father. Now, that they had decided to build. They were anxious to get started, and it happened one day.

The children loved to watch the carpenters as they hammered and sawed that summer. They had never had so many blocks and chips to play with in all their lives.

During this time, one of the carpenters got married. He took a lot of good-natured ribbing from his friends and the Fox men. One day while he was cementing the back porch, Edith started teasing him too. When he smoothed the cement, he used a patting motion. "Now, you are slapping your wife," she teased. A slight grin on his face heightened her fun, so she continued. "Now, you are slapping her again," teased Edith, as he patted down the cement. "You should not do that," she reproached him.

"Edith!" came Lydia's voice from the inside of the house, where she had been eavesdropping. When Edith entered the house, Lydia reproved her sharply. "You should be ashamed of yourself, talking like that to John." When Mother came home from shopping, she gave Edith a scolding too.

Edith could not understand why it was all right for grown-ups to tease, but wrong for children. Grown-ups could do everything. Why couldn't she ever be a grown-up, she wondered, but she stayed away from the carpenters after the scolding. She did not want to do anything wrong again.

The carpenters built a sink that had two faucets. One had cold water, but the other one held water that had already been heated in a large tank behind the stove. Edith no longer had to fill the reservoir. There were two deep dish pans built into the sink, below the faucets. One was to wash the dishes and one was used to rinse them. After the dishes were done, a hole in the sink could be opened and the water disappeared all by itself. The carpenters constructed lots and lots of cupboards. That kitchen was enormous. At last the carpenters were finished and Mother had her roomy kitchen to work in. She was happy, but Father had needs too.

"I just have to have another horse," he told Mother one day. "I can't use Charlie at all anymore, and Dewey is getting too old to help with the farm work and pull the carriage too. Everyone is growing so fast, the load is getting heavier all the time."

Shortly afterward, he came home from a sale with Roy. Roy was wild. Edith was afraid of him. She could tell Father was too. Nevertheless, he hitched Roy to the carriage and drove him around for a whole afternoon in an effort to tame him.

Then one Sunday morning, Roy and Charlie had disappeared. Edith was sound asleep, when Father's excited voice awoke her.

"The stable door was open, and they were both gone, when I got out to the barn," he was telling Mother.

"You know that Charlie can open the door. Do you think it is possible that he let Roy out?"

"Roy was tied, and Charlie was penned in behind the cow stable. I don't see how he could have opened the pen, or how Roy could have become untied. No, I am afraid they have been stolen," mourned Father.

As soon as daylight appeared, they found the horses on a neighbor's farm. Evidently, Charlie had opened the door for himself and Roy, but how Roy's rope became untied remained a mystery.

Father decided Roy needed to be driven to take the shiftiness out of him that day. The grown-up girls were going along to church on this Sunday, for the family was invited to dinner after church, so Roy would have an extra heavy load to pull today, which should tame him down.

Edith watched Roy's ears fearfully that morning. He laid them back on his head. This was a sure sign of his wildness. He shied at bushes and consequently, he almost ran into oncoming cars. He was also acting peculiar with the bit in his mouth.

"Whoa," said Father, as he stopped Roy. Then he handed the lines to Mother, who was sitting on the front seat this morning. He checked Roy's bit to see that everything was all right

"I can't find anything wrong with it," he was puzzled as he climbed back into the carriage, but Roy still acted skittish.

Father sensed there was something wrong, so he stopped Roy a second time, to check his bit. Again he found nothing wrong. It was a new bit, so why should there be anything wrong with it? Then as Father took a step toward the carriage, Roy broke into a startled run. He ran faster and faster leaving Father far behind. The faster the carriage went, the louder Edith screamed. The lines lay useless in Mother's lap, because the new bit had snapped in two. There must have been a fault in it.

As Roy ran he narrowly missed carriages as he passed them. Then he ran up an embankment, and the carriage upset. He dragged it a few feet before he broke loose.

Then Edith saw blood running down Mother's face. Lydia and Mary Ann were scratched and Edith's body was bruised. Emma and Alice were crying. Everybody was bloody and dirty. Soon a crowd gathered at the accident. A car stopped and took the family to the doctor.

Mother's face needed stitches, but miraculously, no one else was seriously hurt. There were only scratches and bruises.

Someone caught Roy and took him to a farmer's barn, until Father could claim him. Father did not want to see him again. He sold him without bringing him home.

With Charlie it was a different story. Father loved that old horse. Charlie had served him faithfully for many years. Now he was old and could no longer work.

"Why don't you sell him to the horse scavenger?" Harvey wanted to know.

"I simply can't do that," replied Father.

"Then you could shoot him and put him out of his misery. He is so old and itchy."

"I can't shoot him either," mourned Father. "He seems like one of the family, but sometime when I am not at home, you may shoot him and bury him in the corner of the upper field."

A few months later, Father came home one day and Charlie was missing. Father asked no questions, but tears rolled down his weathered face.

Chapter 9

Adventures

One Sunday afternoon Anna Nolt had a party and invited the school girls. They were having so much fun playing with the unhitched carriage.

Anna's parents drove a carriage, like Edith's parents did, but many of the other children's parents owned cars, so riding in a carriage was a novel experience. A few girls sat in the carriage, while others pulled the carriage. Edith was standing between the wheels ready to step into the carriage when the girls began to pull. The carriage knocked Edith down, and then drove over her.

The next day, Edith's insides were so sore, she could hardly walk, but she was afraid to tell her parents. She knew she should not have been standing between the carriage wheels. She hurt enough; she did not want to be scolded too. And the soreness went away in time.

Another time, she would have been glad if Mother would have been there to scold her, she was that scared. It all happened because Edith and Henry were alone. Father, Mother and Lydia were at a funeral. They had taken Emma and Alice along, because they were too small to be left with Edith and Henry, and the older boys were working in the fields, so Edith and Henry were in the house all by themselves.

They were playing upstairs, when suddenly, they became aware of a noise downstairs. They looked at each other in fear.

"I am going down there and see who is there," Henry whispered.

"Don't go, they might kill you." Edith's eyes were big with fright.

"I am going down," Henry repeated in a whisper, and he sneaked across the room and crept down the steps.

Edith was too scared to stay upstairs all by herself, so she followed. She held tight to Henry's shirt as they neared the bottom steps. The noise was louder now. She was scared to go on, but she was more scared of being alone.

"I am going to open the door," Henry whispered, but his face was white and scared.

"No, don't," begged Edith. She should have known better. Begging only edged Henry on. His hand took hold of the knob and opened the door a tiny crack. Even so, somebody fell against it. Edith ran back upstairs, screaming, but Henry pulled the door shut, before he fled upstairs after Edith. Nobody came after the children, but the scary noise continued.

The scared children stayed upstairs, speaking only in frightened whispers. They watched out the upstairs window. Everything in the yard looked perfectly safe and normal, but the noise continued.

At last, the familiar figure of Dewey pulled into the driveway with the carriage, and in it Father, Mother, and the girls. Henry ran down the steps, laughing and hollering as if he had never heard the word "fear."

Edith followed cautiously behind. Lydia's jacket lay on the floor, outside the stair door. It had fallen from its hook on the door, when Henry had opened it earlier, giving the children the illusion of a person stumbling against it. The noise had been coming from the new water heater that had been installed when the kitchen had been enlarged. The water pipes ran through the back of the kitchen range to heat the water. Sometimes this water became excessively hot and boiled, creating a scary crackling noise. This is what the children had heard.

After Henry and Edith were outside, Henry declared, "I knew all the time what that noise was. I was just pretending to be scared." Edith knew better, she knew Henry had been scared.

"You were scared," she answered. To avoid further argument, she ran toward the swings that the big boys had hung in the apple orchard. When Henry realized where she was heading, he started running too.

"I can beat you, you are just a girl," he bragged. Edith did win the race and got the swing. Henry stood there with a surprised look on his face. A girl had beaten him.

Soon Floyd, who had just finished his work, arrived on the scene. He and Henry tried to persuade Edith to take turns on the swing.

"It is my turn now," declared Henry.

"I was here first," answered Edith, swinging happily. She had forgotten all about her scare.

"I am the oldest, so I should have the next turn," argued Floyd. Edith did not dream of giving up that swing. She had never had so much fun in all of her life. In fact, she had never realized before just how much fun that swing could be.

While Henry and Floyd were begging, Edith swung. After awhile the boys began whispering to each other, abruptly they left. It was strange, but suddenly, Edith was tired of swinging. It was no longer any fun. Floyd and Henry had gone behind the barn, so Edith followed them. As soon as she reached the corner of the building, both boys who had been hiding there, jumped out and ran for the swing. They grabbed it from opposite sides and jumped on with their bare feet. They stood on it and began to swing together. They laughed and talked about all the fun they were having.

Edith just stared at them. How she wanted that swing back, but she only said, "You can have that old swing. I was tired of it." Then she made a face at them, and ran toward the house.

Chapter 10

Autumn Work

The smell of the good brown earth filled Edith's nostrils as she bent to pick up another potato. Her back hurt so she could hardly bear it, and her arms ached terribly. She had been picking up potatoes since early morning, and she was tired.

Raymond had hitched up Scott, the heavy work horse, to the potato plow and he had plowed up all those potatoes.

Now the family was picking them up. Each person was in a different row. Henry was in the row next to Edith, but he was far behind. Father was on Edith's other side and he was far ahead. He picked so fast, Floyd and John could not keep up with him.

As soon as Edith had filled her bucket, she poured the potatoes in a burlap sack, that had been scattered near each row.

The sun was beating down, relentlessly, and Edith was hot, tired and hurting, but she did not remove her sunbonnet. She did not want to get an ugly sunburn tan or no boy would look at her, she was told. She was not thinking of boys, she was too hungry for that. In fact, she was so hungry her insides hurt, and so tired her outsides ached. She worked slower and slower. Even so, she passed Henry, after she started the second row. She paused long enough to ask him, "What time do you think it is?"

"It must be almost 12 o'clock. I am terribly hungry."

"Why don't you work faster then we will be done sooner?"

"If I work real slow, I don't have to do so much," was Henry's shrewd reply.

"Children, stop talking and get to work, or we won't be done by dinnertime," scolded Father.

"What time is it? I am hungry," said Edith.

Father pulled the leather cord, which was secured to a buttonhole on his trousers. The other side was fastened to his watch, which slid out of his pocket now. "It is nine o'clock," he answered.

Edith could not believe it. "Your watch must have stopped," she told him. Father lifted the watch to his ear.

"No, it is still running. Now, get to work."

Edith was so tired, hungry and stiff, that she could no longer hurry. After she thought at least an hour had passed, she asked Father for the time again.

"Edith, you asked me just ten minutes ago," he replied. It seemed like that morning would never end, but at last they were finished.

Edith was so tired she could not even hurry to get to the table first. Mother and Lydia had prepared a delicious meal, consisting of home baked bread and apple butter, baked beans, mashed potatoes, and a rich brown gravy with lots of meat. There were sour pickles, and chow-chow. For dessert there was a sweet rice pudding, applesauce and pumpkin pies.

Edith ate and ate until she could eat no more. After she was finished eating, Mother said, "Father said you worked real good this morning, so you can rest now. We will do the dishes."

After Edith had rested, she had the whole afternoon to play. First she played with Henry in the barn. They went inside the wheat granary. When Edith stepped into the wheat bin, the wheat tickled her bare feet. Soon she sank into it up to her knees. It was a delicious feeling, and then she saw the mouse.

It just sat there and eyed her. What a nice pet it would make. Henry was in the other bin and did not see Edith's pretty little mouse. Edith started wading toward it, but the mouse did not want to be caught. It hid between a crack in the boards. This crevice was too shallow and the mouse could not get its tail inside. Edith wanted that mouse, so she grabbed its tail and pulled. She pulled and pulled, but the mouse held on. Suddenly, something gave way, and Edith was standing holding the mouse's tail in her hand. She had pulled it right out of the mouse's body. She was glad Henry had missed the whole thing. She never told anyone about the mouse.

Soon Edith was tired of playing in the wheat, so she took Emma and Alice down to the stream in the meadow. The girls were getting bigger now and more fun to play with, and sometimes the stream was just right to wade in.

After a heavy rain the stream became a roaring cascade. At other times it was a mere trickle, but usually, like today, it was a soothing crystal clear stream. As the girls approached, bullfrogs jumped into the water, dragonflies flew over its calm surface and little fish swam in its depth.

Fish would make good pets too, so the girls tried catching them. But the fish darted here and there, now underneath a log, now beneath an over-hanging branch. Suddenly, Alice declared, determinedly, "I am going to catch one," and she reached deep, then lost her footing, and splashed into the stream. She looked so cute, all wet and glittering, with water running off her dress. Edith and Emma laughed and Alice ran into the house for a dry dress.

The next day, the girls were out playing, when an autumn shower came up. Edith watched as the chickens ran for cover.

"It isn't going to rain very long," she predicted.

"How can you tell?" demanded Emma, who was getting wet.

"Oh, I just know about such things," answered Edith, smugly.

"You don't."

"Do so."

"Don't"

"See, it stopped raining, just like I told you it would."

"You can tell me how you knew, without sticking your nose in the air like that," replied Emma, rudely.

Edith was so eager to show off her knowledge that she ignored Emma's tone of voice. "When it is going to rain for a couple of hours, the chickens put their beaks on top of their tails, and take grease from a grease pot, that they have there. They grease their feathers, so they do not get wet."

But Emma was not quite convinced. "How do they know if it will be a short shower?"

"The Good Lord made chickens smarter than people, in this way, so we have to watch the chickens," observed Edith.

Edith had this afternoon to play, but she knew this playtime could not last much longer as the tobacco was just about ready to harvest. Sure enough, the next Saturday Edith and Henry had to go along out to the tobacco field to help the men. They were not strong enough to help cut and string up the big stalks, but they could drop the wooden laths at every fourth stalk. Sometimes they separated the bundles of laths, so they wouldn't be as heavy. But usually Henry took the whole bundle, so he would be done sooner.

He grumbled as he worked. "I don't see why people think they have to chew tobacco. It just makes more work for us, and it takes more of their money. I don't believe it tastes that good anyway." But Henry was curious. He wondered how that tobacco did taste. So when no one was looking, he put some of that green uncured tobacco in his mouth and chewed. He became violently sick and he was white as a sheet. "I will never chew tobacco again as long as I live," he said, after he was feeling well enough to speak.

After the tobacco had all been sheltered in the big barn, the children gathered walnuts that had fallen from the trees. They removed the green outer shell that stained their hands. After this outer shell had been removed they laid the nuts out in the sun to dry. In a few weeks, the walnuts were ready to crack open and eat.

So one day Floyd, Edith, Henry and Emma were in the barn cracking walnuts. They put the nutmeats in a jar, so Mother could use them to bake a walnut cake. They were sitting in a circle, cracking nuts and talking.

"Fancy people are strange," observed Floyd. "They always say 'please' and 'thank-you.'"

"I wonder why they do this. So many extra words would make me tired," Henry replied, as he popped another nut into his mouth.

"Stop eating or we will never get enough shelled for a cake," scolded Edith.

"I am not eating anymore than you are," argued Henry, forgetting all about how tiring extra words were.

"You are so," retorted Edith.

In back of the children was a door that could be opened. It was used to drop straw bales into the barnyard, and it was supposed to be locked.

As the argument heated, Emma squirmed against this door, which was not locked. Suddenly, it flew open and Emma dropped out of sight. Abruptly, the argument ceased and everybody was deadly silent. Then they all screamed, but were still too scared to move.

When they heard the house screen door slam, and heard Mother hollering for help they knew help was on the way. Then they ran down the steps that led to the barnyard below. Emma did not move, and she was terribly white. Her eyes were shut. Someone called the doctor. When he arrived they moved her into the house.

After a while she opened her eyes and smiled. It was the most beautiful smile Edith had ever seen. The doctor said that Emma had only had the wind knocked out of her. She would be all right.

Chapter 11

Farm Animals

Ever since Roy's departure and Charlie's death, Father had been looking for a driving horse. Then one day he came home with Jerry. Jerry was a beautiful dapple brown horse.

Edith was setting the table for supper when Father drove into the driveway, Dewey was hitched to the trotting buggy (another name for the topless buggy) and Jerry was tied to the back of it. "You stay here and help me. You can see that horse after supper," said Mother when she saw Edith was preparing to run outside.

At the supper table Father explained all about Jerry. "Jerry had been a race horse, but he wasn't quite good enough for the track."

"In that case, he should have a little more speed than Dewey had," replied Mother.

"Dewey is old," defended Father.

"I hope he will turn out better than Roy did," remembered Mother.

"I think he will. He has a better reputation than Roy had," was Father's reply.

Nevertheless, after the experience with Roy, Edith was afraid of Jerry. Dewey was the only horse she trusted.

The first time father was driving Jerry, Jerry suddenly pricked up his ears, and broke into a fast trot. Father tightened the lines, but Jerry only gathered more speed.

"Now what caused that," exclaimed Father in amazement, as he pulled harder on the lines.

"There is another team in back of us, and they are trying to pass us," observed Mother. Then Father laughed.

"I've got a race horse here. I will have to remember that." Soon the team in back of them realized they could not pass, and they slowed down. Jerry relaxed somewhat, but he kept his ears pricked, listening for the other horse's feet. He was not going to let that other horse pass him.

All his life with the Fox family, Jerry wanted to race any horse that tried to pass him. Father did not think it was proper for an old man like himself to race with other teams, especially when those other teams were driven by young folks. Sometimes temptation got the best of him, and then he let Jerry run. How Edith enjoyed those times. She knew Father was secretly proud too. Although Jerry could not win a race on the track, he could outrun almost any horse around Lancaster County.

Jerry had also been a riding horse. Whenever he caught a glimpse of any horse with a rider on, he would immediately shift to his riding gait. For a few moments the carriage would be pulled in short unsteady jerks, until Father could pull back on the lines, and get Jerry to revert to his carriage trot.

Just as Jerry had his own personality, so did the heavy work horses. Of all these horses, Barney's peculiarity proved the most interesting.

One day, Lloyd, a neighbor, asked to borrow a horse to plow his lot. Since Barney was the lead horse, Father gave him Barney. The Fox family had just finished their noon meal, when Lloyd came back leading Barney. Lloyd had a worried expression on his face.

"He worked fine this morning, but now he is sick. He seems to be in a lot of pain. I hope it is nothing I did," Lloyd said in a troubled tone.

"Were you trying to finish the lot, before going in to dinner?" asked Father.

"Why yes, as a matter of fact, I was. But what has that got to do with his being sick?"

"Everything," replied Father. "When 11:30 comes around, Barney wants to be fed. He will not work until he gets his food, then he will work again."

"No, I really think he is sick," replied Lloyd. "You can see he is in a lot of pain. You had better get the vet to look at him."

But Father knew Barney. He fed him, and used him in his own field that afternoon. He was not sick at all.

The family dog had a personality too. Sporty was an Airedale. Sometimes he was friendly, but most of the time he was grouchy, even to the family. The boys loved to tease him, because he growled so easily. This teasing made him more disagreeable. He only obeyed Father and Edith.

Every evening before going to bed Father or Edith tied Sporty to the barn so he would not roam and get into trouble during the night. Sporty would not come to be tied when the boys called him, he just growled at them.

Edith was proud that Sporty obeyed her, but one day he refused to come to be tied when she called him. A few days later he disobeyed Father, and only growled when he called. Father knew something had to be done.

During this period, Uncle Will, who raised chickens, had problems with chicken thieves. He offered to take Sporty, then he kept him tied to the chicken house. The stealing came to an abrupt halt. Sporty, with his mean disposition had a use after all.

Edith missed Sporty, so when Father came home one day with a little black ball of fur, her joy knew no bounds. After Sporty, this puppy seemed so friendly.

Trixie loved the whole family, and they in turn loved

him. It did not take long until he could play tug-of-war with Edith. She would hold onto one end of a knotted burlap sack. He would grab the other end, and they both would pull. Trixie was strong but Edith was stronger. As soon as he realized she was pulling him to her side, he would begin shaking the sack. He would shake and shake until her hold loosened. Then he would take a firm grip with his mouth and jerk the sack out of her hands, and run. He could outrun Edith but she could outwit him. She would grab one end of the sack, and the game would start all over again.

There were also cows on the farm, but they had no names. The front cow was black and white and gave a lot of milk. The tan cow did not give as much milk, but there was more cream in her milk. The brown and white cow dripped milk from her udder as soon as she saw the men come with the milk buckets.

The men gave milk from the black and white cow to the cats, because it was not as rich with cream. The cats did not need all that cream, because they were supposed to catch rats and mice to supplement their diet.

Of all the animals on the farm, Edith loved the kittens best. There were lots of cats that had lots of kittens for Edith to play with. The only problem was finding them.

Every evening, when the men were finished with the milking, they filled a bowl of milk for the cats. Edith and Henry watched the cats. If a cat looked thin and undernourished and had been suckled, they knew she had kittens.

Then they waited until she left the bowl and followed her at a distance. Usually she would disappear behind a straw bale and was gone. All the cats were good escape artists, but sometimes the children were lucky and they were able to follow a mother to her nest.

Henry loved outsmarting the cats, but Edith loved playing with the kittens. What an enjoyable afternoon she would have playing with those cuddly kittens. The next morning to Edith's distress the kittens would be gone. The mother had hidden them again. Sometimes, because Henry liked the hunt, he would help Edith find those kittens again.

As the kittens grew older they would come to the bowl by themselves. Then the mother cat no longer hid them. When they were this age, Edith, Emma and Alice spent many happy hours with the kittens. They dressed them in doll dresses, and pushed them around in the doll carriage.

One small kitten was especially receptive to this form of play. The girls called her Tiny, because she stayed little. When the other kittens grew tired of being held, Tiny just purred and purred.

Chapter 12

School Fun

$\mathcal{E}$ dith remembered that strange walk her parents had taken in the middle of a very busy week. She now knew they had been discussing the possible buying of a farm that a neighbor had for sale. They didn't want the children to go along and ask questions. That walk did not seem so mysterious now.

Father bought the farm for David. The former owner was having a sale on this day to sell his farm implements. Edith loved sales, because Mother usually gave the children a nickel to spend at the sale. Today was a special day and a special sale because Edith's parents now owned this farm. Edith understood how special it was when Mother handed each child ten whole pennies.

At the sale there was a long stand filled with candies. Edith bought a stick of chewing gum with one of her pennies. The gum was delicious, so she used her other nine remaining pennies for nine more pieces of gum. She was afraid of losing the gum so she ran across the street with it. Father was home at that moment.

"You spent all your money on gum!" Father was shocked that Edith would spend money on something as useless as gum. "You can't eat it or wear it," he began, but Mother interrupted.

"Let her be, if that is what she likes." Edith was glad for Mother that day. She saved her from a scolding. That sale was on a Saturday, and the gum lasted almost all week. Edith loved having gum in school. In fact she also loved school without gum. She loved every single day of it, and she loved Fridays best of all. Fridays were fun days. Almost every Friday after the last recess, Mr. Wenger would say, "Boys and girls, put your books away. We are going to have a Geography Match today." Then he would choose two of the older students to be leaders. These leaders stood on the opposite sides of the room. They took turns choosing children they wanted on their teams.

After everyone was chosen Mr. Wenger said, "Mary, you may begin."

"Lancaster County," began Mary. Then the turn went to the first person on the opposite side. A place must be chosen that begins with the last letter in the first word.

"York."

"Kutztown."

"New Holland."

"Delaware."

"Lester, it is your turn," said Mr. Wenger, when Lester did not give the name of a place.

"I know, but I can not think of a place," answered Lester.

"You need an E. You can surely think of an E." But Lester could not think of one place that began with an E.

"One minute is all you get. Time is up. Take your seat. Next."

"Ephrata." Edith was glad she had thought of a town as near as Ephrata. It would have been terribly embarrassing to miss it. But now they had an A. A's were hard to get rid of.

"Atlanta."

"Alabama."

"Arizona."

"Akron." Everybody breathed a sigh of relief. They had finally gotten away from the A. Soon most of the familiar places were taken. One by one the children dropped out of the game, because they could not think of the name of a place. Mary's side won the game, because they had someone on their side that could think of a name more often than the other side could.

Sometimes they had spelling matches, where the children had to spell a word that Mr. Wenger pronounced for them. One day Mary Brubaker was reading a library book, when Mr. Wenger announced, "Today we are having a spelling match."

Mary loved spelling matches, but on this particular day, she wanted to finish the book she was reading. When her name was called she said, "I don't want to help. I want to finish this book."

"You can read that book any time. Today I want you to help with the match."

Mary stood up and got in line, but she decided that the very first word Mr. Wenger would give her she would spell wrong, so she could sit down and finish her book.

Mr. Wenger knew Mary very well. When her turn came he said "cat." She could not misspell "cat" he thought.

"Cat, K-A-T, cat," Mary spelled. Mr. Wenger had no choice; he had to let her sit down. But he took away the book she had been reading.

Once a year, the Hinkletown School had a Spelling Bee. A few months before the bee was to be held, the children began to study their parts for the program.

This particular year all of Edith's friends were chewing gum. It seemed to be a status symbol, so Edith wanted gum to chew at the Spelling Bee. She knew how Father felt about chewing gum, so she didn't dream of asking him to buy her a piece. She thought of praying for a piece, but she was not sure it was right to pray for something as selfish as gum.

Still she had this strange feeling that the Good Lord knew all about it. Somehow, she was sure He would provide a piece for her. Two days before the Bee was to be held, Mother found that she did not have as much food as usual to put in the children's lunch boxes.

"Here, children, I will give you each a penny, so you can buy something for your lunch. I don't have enough food here today," she said, as she handed each child a penny to spend at the store that was next door to the school.

Edith bought a piece of gum, but she did not chew it. She brought it home and put it in her dresser drawer. She was going to save it for the Spelling Bee.

The day of the Bee, Elam Kreider, the traveling salesman, visited the Fox family. After Mother had bought the things she needed, Kreider handed each of the children a piece of gum.

Edith could hardly believe it. The Good Lord had provided her with two pieces of gum for the Spelling Bee.

Every year these Spelling Bees were held at night. The schoolhouse was not wired with electric, so for this one night they strung extension cords from the store to the school on temporary poles.

The Bees were always well attended because Mr. Wenger knew how to plan a great program. There were usually two spelling classes and one general information class.

Edith loved the three or four plays they performed during the evening. This year Harvey Good was playing the fiddle in one on those plays, when suddenly a black greased man appeared on the stage.

"Why don't you play something nice?" he demanded.

"All right, what shall I play?"

"Old McDonald had a farm."

"I bet he used some of our black grease," whispered Edith.

"Sh, I want to listen."

"I'll play if you will sing," continued Harvey.

So the black man began to sing, "Old McDonald had a farm. E-I-E-I-O. And on this farm he had some hens, E-I-E-I-O, with a GOCK GOCK here and a GOCK GOCK there, everywhere a GOCK GOCK, Old McDonald had a farm, E-I-E-I-O."

"Why you laid an egg," cried the surprised fiddle player. There right behind the singer, on the chair seat lay an egg. He seemed as surprised as the fiddle player was.

"Ah laid an egg?" he asked in disbelief.

"Get a cup. I want to see if it is any good," said the fiddle player. The singer disappeared behind the stove and re-appeared with a cup.

"You hold the cup, while I break the egg," requested the fiddle player. So while the singer held the cup, he went through a spasmodic fit. As he held the cup, he backed further back until the fiddle player was holding the cup by himself, with the broken egg inside.

"Why it's rotten," he exclaimed, and threw the contents over the crowd. The egg had been filled with confetti.

A few weeks after the Spelling Bee was over, the children received the reward for all their hard work. Mr. Wenger bought library books and playground equipment with the money they had earned.

Chapter 13

The Wedding

The dark receded slowly as dawn appeared. Inside the Fox's kitchen, Lydia was busy sweeping the floor with the homemade broom. She sang as she worked. "Blow out the light, Edith," she interrupted her singing. "We don't want to burn a hole in the daylight." Then she went back to her singing.

"I know why you are singing. You are singing because Jake was here on Sunday night," teased Edith.

"Don't you think that is something to sing about?" grinned Lydia. Jake came to see Lydia every Sunday night now, but Edith had no idea what he looked like. He always went to the parlor door from the outside door, and Lydia always kept the door between the two inside rooms shut.

One Sunday evening after Jake had been there awhile, Henry said to Edith, "Let us see if we can make Lydia cross."

Edith did not like when Henry talked that way. It usually meant mischief. Nevertheless, she asked, "How can we do that?"

"We can make up a little song."

"What kind of little song?" Edith wanted to know.

"How does this sound?"

	(Translation)
"Check, beck, hinkle dreck	Jake, bake, chicken dirt,

Bis marr-u free	By tomorrow
Bisht do doe aweck."	You'll be gone.

In Pennsylvania Dutch the last words rhymed.

"We can't do that, Lydia will scold us." Edith did not quite dare to be so bold.

"No, she won't do anything as long as Jake is here, and by tomorrow she will have forgotten all about it."

"I don't think we should," Edith protested.

"Come on. It will be fun." So Edith let herself be persuaded.

They sneaked up the front steps and hid beside the parlor door. Then they sang their little song, softly. Edith expected the parlor door to open any minute. She was ready to run, but nothing happened.

"We will have to sing louder," said Henry. They did, but nothing happened. They shouted still louder a couple of times. After awhile they grew tired of shouting and singing. They left to play.

Next morning, Edith was scolded. She never knew if Henry got scolded. But Lydia and Jake were on their minds a lot, because they had been seeing each other for a couple years now.

"Do you believe she is getting married to Jake?" Edith asked Henry one day.

"I don't know, but Ivan got married, so I guess Lydia can too."

"But why would she want to get married and leave home to go and live with a strange man?" Edith wanted to know.

"Grown-ups are strange that way. You never know what to expect."

Sometime later, Lydia did not go along to church with David and Mary Ann, in the buggy like usual.

"Why isn't she going along to church?" Edith asked Mother. "She always goes to church."

"You shouldn't ask so many questions," Mother admonished, then Harvey snickered and Lydia blushed.

In church, after the sermon was over and everybody was just about ready to leave, the preacher stood up and announced, "David Fox's Lydia and Jacob Weaver's Jacob are intending to become one."

Then the room began to buzz with people's comments. "I knew it. I just knew they were getting published today," although nobody but the immediate families and the bishop had really known. Even the younger Fox children had not been aware of the fact.

When the family got home from church, a strange young man was there. It was Jake and he was staying for dinner. He talked to Father and Mother as if he had a perfect right to be there, but to Edith he was still a stranger who was taking Lydia and she resented him.

The next two weeks before the wedding were busy ones. The first week was spent in cleaning the house, upstairs and downstairs. The second week Father killed ten of his ducks, and the women butchered and dressed them. They cooked and baked from early morning until late at night.

At last Thursday, the day of the wedding arrived. It was a beautiful winter day for a wedding. As soon as breakfast was over and the chores were done, the family all dressed in their Sunday best clothing. Lydia wore her beautiful gray dress (the traditional color for Old Order Mennonite brides). As soon as the guests began to arrive, an usher, a stranger to Edith, stood at the door and showed the guests where to go. The usher directed the unmarried guests upstairs. The married and the older couples stayed downstairs. There was no place to put all those bonnets and shawls downstairs, so the usher carried them upstairs, and laid them on a bed. Soon two beds were overflowing with the wraps of over one hundred and fifty guests.

Edith felt lost in her own home, a stranger among all these strange people. She stayed close beside Mother; so did Emma and Alice. Edith was used to noise and confusion with ten brothers and sisters still living at home, but it was nothing in comparison to this jumble of strange voices.

Soon a strange young man appeared with a tray loaded with tiny glasses. The glasses were filled with different colored liquids. When the stranger offered Edith a glass from that tray, she chose one with pink liquid.

Behind the strange man came a strange lady with a tray of cookies. These were the cookies that Lydia had baked and frosted. They all had white frosting. Some had coconut spread over the frosting; others had a nut pressed into the frosting. They all looked delicious, but Edith chose a coconut one. She felt more at ease, and then she took a swallow of her drink. It made her cough, and it tasted like medicine. All of the strangeness returned.

"Don't you like your wine?" a strange voice asked her.

"No, it tastes horrible," Edith said coughing, and everybody laughed.

"Drink your wine and be quiet," Mother reproached her, so Edith took a swallow of that awful wine, then quickly she took a bite of cookie, to take away that terrible taste and that dreadful urge to cough.

Soon someone motioned to Mother. "You stay here with Fannie and Edna," she told the girls as she left. Fannie and Edna were Father's two married daughters. Edith could not play with their children today, because they were not allowed to come to the wedding. There were no children there except Edith and her brothers and sisters.

After a while, Edith became aware of a strange voice calling familiar names, "Mr. and Mrs. Samuel Sauder," the strange voice said, then Fannie left. Edith and her little sisters crowded against Edna.

"Mr. and Mrs. John Martin," called the strange voice, and Edna prepared to leave. This time Edith tried to follow her.

"Stay where you are. Soon someone will call your name and tell you where to sit," said Edna.

After a while the stranger called Edith and told her where to sit, in her own home. After she sat down she found herself seated between Floyd and Henry. There were rows of strangers in back of her and rows of strangers in front of her. Edith felt so odd in her own home, that her body began to tremble. It shook and shook. She could not stop its trembling. Soon everybody began to sing in German just like they did in church. Then everybody turned toward the stairs, so Edith looked too. Lydia and Jake came down the steps.

Jake had on a dark gray suit with no collar and plain trousers to match, just like Father's. Lydia had on her new gray wedding dress. (There were small samples of that dress and her blue second best dress, pinned together. They were up-stairs in a small glass dish on the bureau. Each guest could take one home for a keepsake.) Now, Lydia and Jake sat down on two empty chairs in the front row.

Chapter 14

The Wedding Continued

As soon as the singing ended, a preacher stood up and delivered the sermon. It sounded just like it did in church and Edith relaxed a little. The trembling slowed then stopped.

While the minister was preaching, Edith heard noises and muffled laughter from the kitchen. Some married neighbors and relatives had been invited to cook, and a handful of unmarried girls had been asked to be table waiters. They were in the kitchen now preparing the noon meal. Edith listened to the kitchen noises. They were less frightening. Then Lydia and Jake stood up, and Edith forgot all about the kitchen noises.

The bishop was speaking now. He was asking them questions, and they were answering yes. Then they held hands, right there, in front of everybody. The bishop put his hand on top of theirs and said, "I now pronounce you man and wife."

The two attending preachers also spoke a few words, agreeing with the bishop's sermon, and the joining of Lydia and Jake. Then the crowd dispersed into other rooms, allowing the cooks and their husbands to set up a long table the whole length of the front room. As soon as the table was in place, the table waiters covered the table with a long white cloth. Then they placed the plates and silverware on the table.

Soon someone began calling peoples names. He did not say Jacob Weaver and Lydia Fox. He said, "Mr. and Mrs. Jacob Weaver." Lydia did not look like Mrs. Jacob Weaver. She looked like Lydia.

Lydia and Jake sat at the end of the table. Jake's family sat on his side of the table, and Lydia's family claimed her side. Father and Mother sat down, then Fannie and her husband. Everybody sat down according to their age.

After a silent blessing, the table waiters served the food. All the food except the cake was on the table. Edith had never seen so much food in all her life. Everybody waited for the table waiters to hand them the dishes of food. They did not reach and help themselves at all. But Edith was in her own home and she wanted a few after dinner mints, so she took the dish and served herself. She handed the dish to Floyd, but the table waiter intercepted the dish and set it back on the table. Then Edith realized she could not serve herself at her own table. These grown-up strangers had more rights in her own home than she had. She was glad that Lydia and Mother had missed her blunder. She did not want to be scolded.

As soon as dinner was over and the long table removed, everybody sat in rows across the room as they had in the morning. The whole afternoon was spent in singing German hymns, with only a short interval to serve cookies and wine.

All day everyone was solemn and dignified, but as soon as the preachers and the married folks went home, there was a noisy stomping of feet. Soon a table waiter appeared, then another and yet another. They were carrying something in their dainty white aprons. They held both bottom corners above their waists. They stepped in front of Lydia and Jake with those bulging aprons. Then they threw open their aprons and confetti flew all over Lydia and Jake. As more and more table waiters unloaded their aprons, the room became a whirlwind of confetti. Soon everyone was throwing confetti at each other. It was the most fun Edith had all day.

"Where did all this paper come from?" Edith wanted to know.

John took time to answer her, "The table waiters and the hostlers tore up all the paper that the gifts were wrapped in, and now it is confetti."

"Oh, then the table waiters and hostlers were not helping to sing. They were tearing up paper upstairs." This time nobody answered her; they were too busy throwing confetti.

At the supper table the table waiters and the hostlers were silly and boisterous. The hostlers removed the plates of the newlyweds and replaced them with a large platter that they had to share. They also removed the water glasses and replaced them with a two-quart glass mason jar.

After supper was over, everyone continued to release their pent-up energies. Now the party games began. In one of those games, the boys had to catch a girl and kiss her. Henry and Edith, who had stayed up late, giggled at the silly things those grown-ups did.

Soon one of the young boys was ready to leave. He handed one of the hostlers a small slip of paper.

"Come on, boys," this hostler said to the other ones. "We have to hitch up a horse."

"What was on that piece of paper?" Edith wondered.

"The hostlers who care for the horses, write a certain number on the horse's harness. They write this same number on the buggy with chalk. Then they write this number on a slip of paper and give it to the driver. When the driver is ready to leave, he gives this slip of paper to the hostler. The hostlers can then find the right horses and the right buggies to go with them."

"You mean, the drivers don't unhitch their own horses?" asked Edith in astonishment. She had never heard of such a thing.

"That is right. The hostlers do it for him. They also water and feed the horses at noon."

"Wow, I would rather be a driver than a hostler, wouldn't you?"

"I don't know. The hostlers get paid for this. They ask the drivers for money. At first the drivers pretend they left their wallets at home. Then the hostlers pretend to unhitch the horses again. But the drivers always give them money after awhile. I would like to have that money. I could buy a knife with it." All farm boys need pocket knives.

Edith's eyes wanted to close, so she went to bed before the wedding guests left. She had gotten up at four o'clock, and she simply could not stay awake any longer. She fell asleep to the tune of "Skip to Malu, My Darling."

The morning after the wedding, the stillness woke up Edith. "Lydia," she whispered softly. Nobody answered, but Edith knew somebody was in Lydia's bed. "Lydia," Edith whispered louder this time.

"Don't be silly. She is sleeping in the spare room with Jake. She is married now, you know," answered Mary Ann, who had stayed at home for the night, after all the festivities of the day before.

Jake stayed for breakfast too, and then he left. Everything seemed the same as before the wedding, until Saturday arrived. Now that Lydia was married she no longer went along to singings with David. These were only for single adults. Every Saturday evening Jake came and stayed until Monday morning.

Every Sunday morning, Jake and Lydia went to church together. Then they visited friends and relations and stayed for the noon meal. Sometimes they stayed for supper. Usually, Edith's parents with the younger children were also invited for the noon meal. They did not stay for the evening meal because Father had to help with the chores at home.

Chapter 15

Christmas Time

Now that Lydia was married, she needed many things to start housekeeping. It kept Mother and Lydia busy to gather these items.

"Next week we will put a quilt in the frame for you," Mother told Lydia one day. So Father took Mother to buy material for Lydia's quilt. Mother let Edith go along, because she had finished all her work.

When they had finished their shopping, Mother suggested, "We could drive over to your brother Dan's place and invite Ella to the quilting, then we won't have to make a special trip." So Father turned Jerry toward Uncle Dan's house. When they arrived, Aunt Ella was busy baking Christmas cookies.

Nevertheless she urged, "Do stay awhile, since I don't see you often." So Father tied Jerry under the shed roof, and they all went into the house.

"We can only stay a little while, since it is almost time to start the feeding and the milking," said Father.

"If you don't get home in time, your boys will start the chores, so there is no need to rush off," answered Aunt Ella.

"I am sure they would begin the chores, but I promised to be home in time to do them myself."

"That was a promise you should not have made. But it is near Christmas, so I will not hold a grudge. I won't even let you go home without giving Edith a small Christmas gift."

Then Aunt Ella opened a closet door and took out a Mother Goose storybook and a whole box of candy.

Edith was delighted and she stammered her thanks. A whole box of candy all for herself. She had never heard of such a thing.

"If you mention the box of candy to Emma or Alice you will have to share with them," Mother told Edith on the way home.

"I won't tell them," Edith decided. It was her candy, and she had no intention of sharing it with anybody. She would read the storybook to them however. She would sneak upstairs when the girls were not looking, and eat a piece of that delicious candy. It was so good that it lasted only a few days, but it would have been better, if she could have told the girls about it. And she did, as soon as she had eaten the last bite. She could not understand why Mother scolded her for this.

Mother had four long straight pieces of wood. This was the quilt frame. She sewed the material that she wanted for the bottom of the quilt to the frame. Then she formed the frame into a square and fastened the corners with clamps. She lifted the frame on chair backs and laid an inside filling on the backing material. On top of the filling, she laid the patchwork top. Now, the cover was ready to be quilted.

Aunt Ella was one of the first quilters to arrive. Soon more quilters arrived. They gossiped as they quilted. Edith did not know there were so many people who did things that were worth gossiping about.

Edith and Emma lay on the floor underneath the quilt. They loved to watch people's fingers from that angle. Or they stood and watched Aunt Ella's face. When she stuck the needle into the material she grimaced. She twisted her mouth this way and that way with the rhythm of every stitch she took.

"Is this the way she does it?" Edith whispered to Emma, as she made a face for Emma under the quilt.

"No, that isn't right. This is how you do it," but Edith did not think Emma's face was right either.

While everyone was quilting, Lydia was preparing a cooling drink and some Christmas cookies for the quilters. Lydia and Mother had spent a whole day baking cookies, but when Edith and her younger sisters had wanted to sample the ones that did not get right, Lydia had vetoed the idea.

Edith wished she were a grown-up, and then she could have eaten the first ones that did not get right, because Lydia did not have the dough thick enough. Grown-ups had all the fun.

"If we eat only one cookie each, it will take more than a dozen. So nobody gets any until the quilting," Lydia had said, and Mother agreed. Edith managed to eat three at the quilting without Mother's notice, however.

In the Fox household, Christmas was observed as the Lord's birth. It was celebrated much as the Sabbath was, by church attendance and ceased labor. There was no Christmas trees or Santa Claus; they were wrong. In school, however, there was a lovely tree. Santa Claus was there too, and he gave each child a small box of candy and an orange. The children, with the teacher's help, prepared a program for the parents. They performed short Christmas plays, recited poems and sang carols.

One year after Christmas, when the older students dismantled the tree, Edith gathered all the discarded tinsel. She took it home and decorated the asparagus fern in her bedroom. She loved her Christmas tree, but only a few weeks later Mother removed all her precious tinsel.

Another Christmas, the children pasted together colored paper rings and made them into a paper chain, and hung them across the front room. It made the room look real 'Christmassy.' Christmas Day dawned bright and clear, so the whole family went to church on that day. A preacher, who was not usually in this district, had the morning service. Because he was a distance from home, Father and Mother invited them to dinner. The clergyman and his spouse gratefully accepted this invitation.

When Mother had issued the invitation, she had forgotten all about the decorated front room. When she came home and saw the gaily-decorated room, she was horrified. She did not want the preacher to see how worldly she had allowed her children to become.

"Hurry up, Edith. Get rid of those chains," she hollered. In her attempt to remove them quickly, she grabbed them, tearing them all apart.

"Be careful, Mother," pleaded Edith. "I'll help you. Don't tear them."

Mother did not hear a word of Edith's plea; she was too busy hollering, "Hurry, hurry." She was afraid that Eli Hursh's wife would enter the room before all those strings of rings were disposed of. She finished tearing down the last chain and handed the whole bunch to Edith.

"Hurry, hurry," she cried. Edith ran into the kitchen and slammed the door just as the preacher's wife entered the front room.

In her best company voice Mother said, "Come in, do come in. It is a real pleasure to have you visit us today."

In the kitchen Edith stopped in her tracks, she was utterly amazed. Mother had changed from frantic anger to calm friendliness all in a moment. How could she do that? Grownups always surprised her.

Christmas usually arrived just before the tobacco crop was sold, so Edith's parents were forever short of cash at Christmastime. Still they managed to give each child a big plate of candy and an orange for Christmas each year. About a month after Christmas, the tobacco crop was sold, then the children received their toys.

During the winter of Lydia's wedding there were no toys. All the money was needed for Lydia's household things. Mother and Lydia were always preparing something for Lydia. They bought some of her furniture at public sales. They removed the old paint and refinished it like new. They sewed sheets and pillowcases. They made tablecloths from colored feedbags. Every spare moment was spent in preparation of Lydia's moving. Edith had learned to accept Jake's presence during that winter, but she could not understand how Lydia could leave Father and Mother and the whole family and leave with a stranger.

The last week in March was chosen for their moving day. It would be early enough, so they could prepare a garden and plow the fields for farming, but most of the expense of the winter would be over.

The planned moving day turned out to be gorgeous, weather-wise. Early in the morning, Jake's parents arrived with a big two-horse flat wagon. Father used his big flat wagon too. Some people arrived with smaller spring wagons. Everybody worked swiftly, loading all the furniture that had been stored in the house and barn. The smaller wagons were loaded with household items and the groceries. As soon as everyone was ready, the whole procession drove to Jake's and Lydia's new home.

While the women unloaded the groceries and the cooking utensils, the men set up the cook stove. Soon the busy women had a delicious meal prepared for the hungry workers. After dinner everyone helped until all the furniture was in place.

It seemed strange leaving without Lydia, but Edith had fun riding home on Father's big flat wagon with her younger brothers and sisters.

Chapter 16

A Familiar But Odd Sunday

The summer sun was already high in the heavens, when Father hitched Jerry to the carriage. It was a beautiful Sabbath day. Jerry stepped briskly as they headed for church this morning. The family was going to the Groffdale Meetinghouse. This was where Lydia and Jake attended now that they had moved.

As they neared the church, they saw teams coming from every direction. These horses made Jerry quicken his pace. Many horses tried to pass the Fox carriage, but Jerry would not allow them to do this.

At the Martindale Church, where the family usually attended, Edith still sat with Emma and her little friends, to keep Emma from crying. Silently Edith was rebelling, for she did not want to sit with the little girls. Now, Emma was standing at Edith's side, but her attention was diverted by a crying baby. Edith noticed the girls her own age were forming a line and filing into the main room (or sanctuary). Quickly Edith stepped in the line and filed in with the other girls. She took a seat in the middle of the bench. Other girls filled the bench. There was no room for Emma.

Emma was still absorbed in the baby. Suddenly, she seemed to realize Edith was no longer there. She scanned the room in fright. Her eyes found Edith in the main room. They were pleading and full of tears. Edith turned her head away. When she looked again, Emma was sitting in the main room with girls her own age. Although Mother scolded Edith later, when Emma told her what she had done, Mother did not insist that Edith sit with her again.

After the meeting was over, Mother and the girls spoke with Lydia. She and Jake were invited to one of Jake's relatives. But the Fox family did not go home. They were invited to dinner at someone else's house.

These people had other company too. One family had a little girl along. She was the prettiest little thing Edith had ever seen. She had the bluest eyes and beautiful golden curls. She wore a fluffy pink dress with a fluffy bow in back. On her tiny feet she had white shoes and white anklets trimmed in red. She was so beautiful she looked like a little angel.

Edith could not take her eyes off little Ann. She felt ugly, awkward and clumsy beside such a vision in such a dress. Edith thought that this must be how angels look, so lovely and pure.

The little girl did not act like an angel. She wanted to go out to the kitchen where the host mother was preparing dinner.

"No, you cannot go out to the kitchen. You will be in the way," her mother told her. Then little Ann began to scream and struggle to get away from her mother. She pouted and cried. She threw herself on the floor. Alice, Emma and Edith just stood there and stared. They could hardly believe their eyes. Ann looked so pure and innocent and beautiful. How could she be so bad.

"Look! The girls are watching you. They never saw such a naughty girl before," said her mother. Ann kept right on screaming until her mother released her. Then she headed for the kitchen.

"Edith, why don't you go and play with Ella?" Mother asked. Edith knew she had been staring, and this embarrassed Mother. She looked at Ella, who was the daughter of the host family. Ella returned her look.

"You could go and play with your wagon," suggested Ella's mother.

"Come on! Let's go!" Ella ran out of the house and Edith followed her.

Edith could think of nothing but that beautiful girl. "I never saw anyone so beautiful," she told Ella.

"Gee whiz, she is a spoiled brat. She just screams until she gets her own way."

Edith could not believe her own ears. She must have misunderstood. Ella could not have used such bad words as "Gee Whiz."

"What did you say?" she asked.

"Gee whiz, she is a spoiled brat. She should be spanked," repeated Ella, heartily. Edith decided Ella must really hate lovely Ann to use such bad words, so she changed the subject.

"Are you in fifth grade in school?" she asked.

"Gee whiz, no," exclaimed Ella, loudly. Ella had done it again. Edith stood there shocked and stared at her. Father would never allow her to use such words.

"Gee whiz, don't look at me like that. I am telling you the truth. I know I am big enough to be in fifth grade, but I didn't pass last year. Gee whiz, I don't care," she finished.

"Oh," replied Edith, subdued. Every time Ella spoke she said Gee whiz. It was frightening to Edith who had been taught such words were wrong. Surely Ella and her family did not attend the Old Order Mennonite Church. Nobody there used such awful words. Edith had heard so many Gee whizzes; she could stand it no longer.

"Do you go to our church?" she asked her timidly.

"Gee whiz, yes," was the boastful reply. Edith asked no more questions. She did not want to hear, Gee Whiz, in that awful tone of voice again.

Edith was glad when it was time to go home at last. At home everything was so familiar and normal, as they sat down to the evening meal. Harvey, who now worked for a farmer, was home for the weekend. The other boys at home included Raymond, John, Floyd and Henry. Mary Ann, Edith, Emma and Alice completed the children. With Father and Mother, there were now only eleven members left in the family. The others were married.

When Lydia and David had still lived at home there had been thirteen, which meant they had to cut one large pie in seven pieces. Someone had to take a smaller piece for dessert. Now everyone could have a regular piece of pie.

This Sunday, Harvey was at home and talking about the farmer he worked with. But Edith was thinking about her day. She found she wasn't very hungry. She was finished first, so she sat back on the settee. She was deep in thought, when she realized Harvey was making strange silent motions to her. Then he looked at Mary Ann and back at Edith to see if she understood. She interpreted his motions quickly. She smiled and nodded her head. Harvey wanted her to tie Mary Ann's apron strings to the chair back, so that when Mary Ann got up, the chair would get up with her.

Edith stole behind Mary Ann's chair and knelt down. Ever so gently, she pulled at Mary Ann's apron strings to loosen them. Harvey kept Mary Ann talking while Edith tied the strings to the chair. The whole family saw what was happening and they helped to keep Mary Ann's attention diverted. All of that attention did not deceive Mary Ann. In fact, it made her suspicious.

"What is going on?" she asked. She looked around and behind her chair.

"Oh, I see what you are doing, Edith, you can stop now," she laughed.

It was all so wonderful and cozy, having fun at home with the family. There were no beautiful children screaming to have their own way, and there was no one rudely saying, Gee Whiz.

Chapter 17

Misunderstandings

S ummer days were busy days on the farm, one right after the other. Inside the house, Mary Ann, who was staying home this summer, was Mother's helper now that Lydia had moved. Mary Ann and Mother did not work together as well as Mother and Lydia had. They were like two horses, hitched together, and pulling in opposite directions.

Mary Ann had been nine years old when Father had married Mother, but Mary Ann could not forget her own Mother. She resented her stepmother taking over the house.

Mother, on the other hand, felt she should train Mary Ann as she would her own daughter. Thus friction arose.

Father tried to keep peace between his loved ones, but when all else failed he retired to the barn.

Mary Ann did not work as fast nor as easily as Lydia had, so Edith had to help more, thus she was caught in the middle with no place to retreat. She had never been physically as strong as most of the other family members. The strain of not taking sides was too much for her. Then on top of everything else her body began to grow rapidly, throwing her off balance. When she reached for a glass of water, her hand reached further than it had before. It knocked the glass over, spilling its contents.

Soon she developed an illness, known as St. Vito's Dance. As this condition worsened, bed rest was ordered by the family physician.

So Edith rested downstairs in her parents' bed during the day, so she would be near the kitchen where Mother could hear her when she needed something. At night she slept upstairs in her own bed.

Everything upset Edith that summer. When she called for Mother, and Mother did not answer immediately, she developed crying spells that left her weak and nervous. Mother made an effort to spend more time with Edith. She bought her a little bell to ring when she needed something.

On the last day of school each year the pupils had a picnic in the woods with food and games. This year Edith could not attend because of her illness, but Floyd came home with a box of goodies just for her. That night Alice, who still slept downstairs in a small bed, ate some of Edith's goodies. Next morning, Edith, forgetting all the good things left, developed another crying spell.

Sometimes, during other nights, she would wake up, and see the moon cast weird shadows on the bedroom wall. She was sure these shadows were murderers or at least thieves, and she was too scared to move. Sometimes she ran downstairs and sat on the chair that was in her parents' bedroom, just to get away from those shadows who seemed to be real people.

Frequently, when she was downstairs, she heard wild dogs outside, at the bedroom window, trying to get in. They growled every time she took a breath. She tried breathing softly, but the dogs heard her and growled. Many years later Edith realized she had heard her Father snore and not wild dogs growling at all.

Edith had not completely recovered from her illness by the time school opened again, but the doctor allowed her to return to school. At times when things did not go her way, Edith still got those nasty crying spells. One day, Mother wanted her to wear a certain sunbonnet to school. Edith despised this bonnet. She thought it was ugly. She was ashamed to wear it. Mother refused to give in to Edith. A crying spell resulted.

On the next doctor's visit, he demanded an explanation about her worsened condition. Edith did not want to be naughty and disagreeable, but she had no self-control.

One day she was filling the water glasses at the table and spilling water at every glass. "Edith," Father suggested, "take it easy. Don't hurry. Hold the pitcher perfectly still before you start to pour."

Edith tried to still her trembling hand. The harder she tried to concentrate, the more her hand shook.

"That is all right. You may finish now," Father said gently. He never referred to the incident again, but Edith knew she had disappointed him.

Some time later, Edith, in a restless mood, found a beautiful doll hidden among Mother's possessions. Since she was the sick girl, she knew the doll was for her. She was too impatient to wait for that doll and she wanted it now. So she simply told Mother that she had found it.

"That doll is not for you, Edith. It is for Emma. You know you never play with dolls."

"I would if I had a nice one. I just have Lydia's old one," she complained because she was very disappointed. But her health was improving, so she could handle frustration better now.

In fact, she found some advantages in the situation that had developed between Mother and Mary Ann. Mother did not require her to obey Mary Ann, as she had insisted on obedience to Lydia. Even so, Mary Ann did not take her frustration out on the children; she often bought toys and other gifts for them.

There were two houses on the Fox property, the big farmhouse where the family lived, and a smaller house that was the "Doddy House." Father and Mother would live in it when they retired, but right now it was rented out to an older couple. This couple had two boarders living with them. One of these was a widow, and the other one was a maiden lady. Annie Martin, the maiden lady, was a handy seamstress.

One day, after a brief chat with Annie, Mother announced to Edith. "I paid Annie to teach you and Emma to hand sew a quilt. Every girl should know how to hand sew, and since I have so much other work to do, Annie said she would teach you for me."

So, Edith and Emma spent a whole hour every day, except Sunday, at the neighbors learning how to hand sew a quilt. Annie was a strict seamstress; she demanded a backstitch for every third stitch. She did not have much patience with the rowdy, noisy Fox girls, and they, on the other hand, had very little patience with her strictness. But Annie had been paid in advance, so she and the girls had to make the best of the situation no matter how much they disliked it.

One day, near the end of the sewing sessions, Annie asked the girls to play more quietly at home. Their loud noise disturbed her afternoon nap.

Edith told Henry what Annie had said, and Henry was happy, "Let's sing and laugh real loud to make her cross." Edith did not need to be asked twice. Every afternoon, Edith and Henry stood at the fence that separated the two houses, playing and laughing loudly to harass Annie. They were careful that their parents did not catch them in this mischief.

One day Annie retaliated. Mother had told the girls to pick the dried navy beans that had grown in the truck patch during the summer. She had handed Edith a brown burlap sack to fill with the beans. Emma and Alice, being so young, soon grew tired of picking beans, and they begged Edith to quit picking.

"We have to pick more than this or Mother will send us right back out," she told them. At last the bag was almost full, although they had picked only half of the row. Still Edith thought, perhaps they might have picked enough to satisfy Mother.

But when they got back to the house Annie was there. "Oh, are you finished already?" asked Mother in surprise.

"Well, no not quite," Edith admitted slowly, but she added quickly, "we did pick a whole lot."

"Yes, you did," admitted Mother.

"I would not let them quit until they are done. They will never learn to obey you, if you don't send them right back out," declared Annie, who had never married and had no children.

"I am afraid Annie is right, girls," agreed Mother. "Go out and finish picking."

"Mother would have let us go if Annie had kept her mouth shut," declared Emma.

Edith knew Emma was right. She also knew she deserved Annie's revenge, but the younger and innocent girls did not. They were suffering too, so Edith said, "I will tell you a story." Edith was a great storyteller, and the girls soon forgot their grievance.

Sometimes they also forgot they were picking beans and stopped to listen to the story. Then Edith would stop talking, sometimes in the middle of a sentence. The girls would grin sheepishly, and resume their picking. It was amazing how fast those beans got picked.

When the girls returned to the house with their bag stuffed, Annie was no longer there.

Chapter 18

A Typical Monday

As Edith grew older she was given more chores to do. Early every Monday morning, she filled a bucket with rain water from the pump which was now in the kitchen and carried it into the adjoining wash house and emptied the water into the big iron kettle that hung over the fireplace. Back and forth she went until she had filled the kettle to the brim. Then she stuffed paper and wood chips into the fireplace underneath the kettle. She poured a sprinkle of kerosene over the chips then struck a match to the pile. The blazing fire heated the wash water, while the family ate breakfast.

While Edith washed the dishes Mother sorted the laundry into piles according to their colors. Mary Ann was hired out now, so Edith was Mother's helper.

Mother was fussy with her laundry. She was afraid of tattletale gray. She soaked every load in cold soapy water first. This sudsy water had Clorox added to remove every stain. In addition, Mother used a metal plunger to work the dirt loose from the laundry. After ten minutes of soaking and plunging, she put the load through the wringer into scalding hot water. To the hot water in her Maytag gasoline-powered washing machine, she added a variety of water softeners, laundry soaps and homemade soap chips. After ten minutes of spinning in the machine, Mother put the wash through the wringer and into the first rinse water. She swirled the wash around with her hands to remove all the soapsuds. Then with the wringer she put the wash through to the last rinse water, which was the bluing water.

While all this was going on, one load was spinning in the washer, and one load was soaking in the cold soapy water. If Mother was finished hanging up a load before the next load had been spinning ten minutes, she worked at something else until the next ten minutes were up.

Mother and Edith did the laundry twice a week. On Mondays they usually had between 20 and 25 loads, but on Thursdays there were only 18 to 19 loads. They did not have the extra clothing from the weekend.

During the days that Mother did the laundry, Edith did the morning chores by herself. She swept the kitchen, fetched coal or wood depending upon the season, took out the ashes and filled the lamps and lanterns with kerosene.

When she had finished the kitchen, she swept the porches and walks. Then she went into all the bedrooms and took up all the bed chamber pots and emptied them into the outhouse. Finally, she made the beds. She always let the boys' bedroom for last.

There was a library with hundreds of books in the boys' bedroom. Some of these books had been Mother's books before she was married. Others had been bought at public sales. Mother had even bought some new ones, just for the family to read. (Father was no reader. He rarely read a book, except the Bible.) But Edith was a reader, and so were most of the family. They sometimes shirked their chores to indulge in this pastime.

That library was the reason Edith let the boys' bedroom for last. She dashed through the bed making ritual, then grabbed a book and began to read. After a while Mother realized it was taking Edith longer than it should.

"Edith, did you finish the beds? If not, finish them,

and stop reading." Mother knew Edith's weakness very well because it was her own too.

"I am coming," Edith would answer, but unless Mother's voice sounded very upset, she would finish the chapter she was reading. There was nothing worse than an unfinished book, unless it was an unfinished chapter.

It usually took Mother and Edith all morning to finish the laundry. Sometimes Edith did not even get time to drain the water out of the machine and tubs before dinner.

With their combined efforts, they could have a hot noon meal ready in an hour's time. Mother would start a wood fire while Edith peeled a big kettle of potatoes. They always had one other vegetable and usually canned meat and gravy. They often had sweetened tapioca pudding. There was also fruit and cake or pie, all homemade. Then they always had homemade bread with butter and apple butter.

The afternoon was needed to catch up with cleaning the dirty eggs that had accumulated during the weekend. Edith did not like to clean eggs. It was a slow monotonous job. Sometimes Mother would tell related stories of her childhood at this time. It dulled the edge of Edith's misery.

As soon as the wash was dry, Edith removed it from the lines. Then Mother folded it, and sorted out the pieces that needed to be ironed and mended. There were always lots of men's white shirts to be ironed and lots of men's socks to be mended. Edith always did the ironing, and they did the mending on rainy days. After supper was over and the dishes were washed, it was time to do the milking. Edith helped with the milking now. Twice a day she milked two of the herd of eight cows, by hand.

As soon as Edith was finished milking the cows, she took the milk to the combination milk house and pump house. There she poured the milk into the strainer, which was atop the milk can. The milk flowed into the can, but the dirt particles stayed behind in the strainer. Then Edith washed the strainer and the buckets, which finished the milking chores.

Mondays were always busy days, but as soon as darkness fell they put away their work. This time was for relaxation for the whole family. Mother lit the kerosene lamp, and everyone sat around the table with games, jigsaw puzzles, or an unfinished book or the Bible.

Although Edith was growing and helping more with the work, she was still a child and loved to play with the other children. Sometimes they played hide and seek in the darkened front room. When the dark green blinds were drawn no outside light could enter the room.

Tonight, Edith took the first turn to be "it." She stayed in the kitchen while the others hid in the darkened room. They would stand behind chairs or anything else that was there. Sometimes they even stood in the middle of the room. When they hollered, "Ready," Edith opened the door and closed her eyes until she had shut the door again, so she could not see anyone from the light that was shining in the kitchen. To begin her search in the darkened room, Edith stretched her arms as far apart as possible, so her hands could explore the space in front of her. She took slow cautious steps. She did not want to bump into furniture, and she did not want to miss anyone.

Soon her seeking hands caught someone that giggled. He wore trousers, but he was shorter than Floyd and John, and he giggled like Henry.

Edith wanted to be sure, so she felt his short hair and small ears. "It is you, Henry," she said. Henry gave her his hand, and they continued the search together. They soon found Emma. She gave her hand to Edith and the three continued their search in the dark. As soon as everyone was found they started another game. Henry was, "it," because they had found him first. One evening, they were playing this game and Henry hid behind the heavy green blind on the windowsill. Although they all searched for him, they could not find his hiding place. He had to tell them where he was.

The children enjoyed playing another game sometimes. It was a word game and had to be played in the lighted kitchen. "It," spelled a word or said a number that could be found somewhere in the kitchen. The rest of the children hunted for this word. Favorite words were the ones that were in small print on calendars on the wall or serial numbers on the back of something.

Edith loved being "It," and the children asked, "Who is the hottest now?" meaning, who is the nearest?

"Floyd is the hottest." So everyone crowded around Floyd.

"Who is the hottest now?" asked Emma, who hoped she was on the right side of Floyd. She placed her hand on a book on the table for support, so she would not be pushed aside.

"You are. You are burning your hand," and she found her word on the book's title.

Another evening when they were playing the word game and eating crackers, one of them came up with the letters, K-R-I-S-P-Y.

Edith asked the all-important question first, "Who is the hottest?"

"Alice is the hottest," and everyone crowded around Alice. She finished her cracker, but did not go for another one. She was too busy searching for the word. Henry went for another cracker.

"Who is the hottest now?" he asked.

Everyone including Henry was surprised when the answer was, "You are." He ate his cracker and found he was no longer the hottest. It turned out to be a confusing game until one of them discovered where the word had been found.

At eight o'clock Father said, "It is bedtime everyone."

"Already!" Edith could hardly believe playtime was over so soon, but she took her shoes off and put them under the settee. Then she opened the door to the darkened front room, and climbed the steps to her own bedroom. She undressed in the dark, knelt to say her prayers, then jumped into bed. It had been a good day.

Chapter 19

War

In December of 1941, the United States entered into war after the bombing of Pearl Harbor, and Edith entered into the most disrupting period of her fourteen years.

She had loved going to school before the war, but now all Mr. Wenger talked about was the war. Edith hated hearing about that awful war. She wanted to forget it was going on, so in her subconscious she turned him off.

Edith's parents did not believe in taking part in the war in any form, but Mr. Wenger's church, (a liberal Mennonite group) obtained permission from the government to set up conscientious objectors' camps near hospitals and mental institutions. From these camps, the men served as helpers at the hospitals.

"It is simply stubbornness to go to prison, where you can do no good to anyone, when the alternate service helps the sick," Mr. Wenger believed, but Edith's brother had chosen prison. Edith was torn between Mr. Wenger's belief and her parents' beliefs.

She was not the only one torn between the two positions. No matter whether the conscientious objector chose prison or camp, he served without pay. For this reason the Old Order Mennonite Church felt it their duty to collect money from its members at home to give to these men who were not getting paid, but the church was divided among itself.

"I will not give a penny to help anyone who was too stubborn to help the sick whenever possible, but sat in prison instead where they are doing nobody any good," insisted one group.

"I will not help anyone who went to camp. They are not suffering for their faith. They are taking a vacation and having a good time," insisted the other group.

But the money was collected, and divided between both groups of Old Order Mennonites, although feelings ran high. The emotions among the non-conscientious objector ran much higher, however.

Buggies were no longer safe at night. They were stoned and harassed. Sometimes, they were even stoned during the day if they happened to be on a lonely stretch of road. Obscenities were shouted at them from passing cars. Hardly a day passed without some incident happening.

One day, Edith rode the trolley to Lancaster to do some shopping. While in a store, she sat down in a snack bar to get a root beer float. The waitress ignored her, but waited on other customers. Edith left the store without her float.

There were less helpers at home since the war began, because Father needed a certain number of points for each son at home. These points were obtained by having a certain number of cows, pigs or chickens. So Mother and Edith had to help out in the fields, but they also had problems in the house.

Sugar had become scarce. Finally it was rationed with the use of sugar stamps. Father did not approve of registering for these stamps. "We can get along without sugar," he said, then added, "perhaps, the war will be over soon."

Recipes using sugar substitutes appeared in magazines and newspapers. So Mother and Edith baked pies and cakes with molasses or some other sugar substitute. Cakes flopped but they were eaten anyway.

The bakery in New Holland began selling their left-over sticky bun topping. After the buns had been baked and removed from the pans, the topping that was left in the pans was collected in large containers and sold. This topping tasted like soft taffy and it contained nuts. Mother tried new recipes to use this topping. Every bit that she did not use the children ate like candy. Candy too had become scarce.

During this time, the bakery also sold broken pieces of jellyrolls. The family got along reasonably well with these sugar substitutes, but when Father was offered a sack of black market sugar, he could not resist although the price was very high.

Since the family had no electric, they had a gas-powered washing machine, and soon gasoline was one of those scarce items. For the car owners, car pools became a way of life. For the Fox women however, the old fashioned washboard became a way of life. Mother and Edith took turns at that board.

Edith's arms grew tired from rubbing each piece of laundry back and forth, back and forth, across that board. When Mother was hanging up her load, Edith sometimes skipped some of the back and forth scrubbing. When Mother was in the washhouse, she did not try any omissions, because Mother seemed to have eyes on the back of her head.

Edith's arms ached the next day, but Mother appeared to scrub the laundry so easily. Edith wished she were grown-up so she could scrub easily, without getting aching arms.

Another rationed item was kerosene. So Mother made candles. Edith loved to help with this job. The candle mold had two rows with six holders in each row. Edith would thread a string in each candleholder. She fastened the string to the mold with a stick. Then Mother poured the hot tallow into the mold. After the tallow was cold it would be hard. Mother dipped the mold into hot water, and twelve perfectly formed candles slid out.

But the candles were not safe to use in the barn. Edith and the men learned to milk in the dark.

During this time Edith had a toothache. It was so painful that sleep was next to impossible. Father did not like to take the children to the dentist, because he had unpleasant memories of dental visits during his youthful years. But something had to be done, so he hitched up Jerry and took Edith to Ephrata to the dentist. Many dentists had gone to war, so there were not enough to go around. Edith noticed, as she entered the waiting room, it was filled with waiting patients. When Edith's turn finally came, the dentist was far behind in his schedule. Consequently, he was in a bad mood. When he looked into Edith's mouth his temper changed for the worse.

"There are thirteen teeth in there to be filled, besides the one that hurts you. That one has to be pulled. Doesn't your family ever take you to the dentist?" he finished angrily. He would never understand Father's reluctance to take the children to the dentist. So Edith hung her head and remained silent.

The dentist was rough as he angrily filled seven of Edith's teeth, and gave her some medication to relieve the pain in the other tooth. Two days later he filled six more teeth and pulled the infected one. He was still upset and he took it out on Edith as he worked on her teeth.

"Tell your Father to bring you in every six months from now on," he demanded.

In the carriage, later, Edith repeated what the dentist had said. "You should have asked him, who is the boss?" was Father's reply. Again Edith hung her head and remained silent. Father would never understand the dentist's position. Edith could never bring herself to go to that dentist again. He had been so devoid of sympathy and so extremely rough.

During the war and after the chores were done, the family sat on the porch in the twilight, and watched the fireflies appear with their flickering light. Sometimes the children played tag in the moonlight, while Father and Mother smiled encouragement. In the winter, they played games that required only candlelight.

It took almost four years for the war to end and longer for things to return to normal. The Good Lord had taken care of the Fox family during those years. A feeling of peace enveloped Edith once more.

Chapter 20

Rex and the Tractor

As each son grew up, Father ordered a new top buggy for them. When John got his new top buggy, he started driving Jerry now and then. One day, Father said, "We need another horse. I need Jerry and you are old enough to have your own horse."

So Father and John went horse hunting. They went to public sales and to private owners that had a horse to sell. They found their horse at the New Holland Sales Stables.

Rex was the most beautiful sorrel horse that Edith had ever seen. John was proud of him, but he was a little worried that Rex was two years old and had not been harness broken yet. It was strange that such a handsome animal had not been trained. John began training him the minute he got him home. Rex seemed to know what was required of him, which puzzled John. It did not make any sense. When John told Father this, Father was disturbed too.

"Something doesn't seem quite right here. A harness trained horse demands a better price, so why was he sold as untrained unless—" Father even hated to think about it, but he said it anyway, "unless he is a balker."

A balker is a horse that absolutely refuses to work. Rex did all right for a whole week, and then it happened. John was at a singing and when it was time to go home Rex would not budge. John's friends pushed the buggy until Rex had to take a step, then another and another. After half an hour of pushing the buggy and pulling at Rex's bridle, Rex suddenly sprang forward, almost running down John's friends, but he kept on going until he got home.

Rex was smart enough not to balk at home. John would have left him stand until he would have been ready to move. But he waited to balk until John was somewhere and wanted to leave, then he simply would not move. Every time this happened it was a little harder to get him to move, but John wanted that beautiful horse and still hoped he could cure him of balking. There was no horse around that was so handsome, so John just tried a little harder to break him of the balking habit.

One Sunday morning John asked Edith if she wanted to go along to church with him. It made her feel like a grown-up, so she nodded her head, "yes." Then he said, "I am driving Rex. We will wait until everybody has gone, then if Rex balks we will just sit there until he is ready to move. We can wait as long as he can."

John was right. After the service was over Rex balked for an hour or so, but he got tired of just standing there, so he threw himself on the ground. John and Edith unhitched him and he stood up again. With soft words and little chirping sounds John persuaded him to move, but it was three o'clock when they finally arrived home.

The day Uncle Will's daughter was married, things finally reached a climax. Mother and Father, Edith and the grown-up boys were invited to the wedding. Uncle Will was not an Old Order Mennonite, so this wedding was different from the ones Edith was used to. She was fascinated with everything, especially that beautiful flowery wedding cake that stood in the middle of the table. It interested Harvey too. When only Edith and her brothers were looking, Harvey winked and pretended to cut a piece of that cake with an imaginary knife, then they all had to stifle their giggling.

John had a previous engagement for that evening, so he wanted to leave the wedding early. The only problem was, Rex was not in the mood to pull the buggy. He balked and John could not get him to move. John was in a hurry, so he unhitched him and put him back in Uncle Will's barn. Then he hitchhiked home.

The next morning bright and early, John showed up at Uncle Will's place. He was bound and determined that he would cure Rex of balking, but Rex had other ideas. When John hitched him to the buggy he just stood there. John slapped the lines across his back to get him to move, and Rex threw himself on the ground.

Uncle Will had a tractor, so he said, "I have heard that you can get a balker started by pulling them with a tractor. Do you want me to try it?"

"Go ahead, I don't know what else to do." So Uncle Will got his tractor, while John unhitched Rex. Then Uncle Will tied Rex to the tractor and dragged him. Dragging hurt Rex so he got up and walked patiently behind the tractor. Uncle Will stopped the tractor and untied Rex. John hitched him to the buggy again then tried to get him going, and Rex threw himself on the ground again. So John unhitched him and Uncle Will tied him to the tractor again. As soon as he started the tractor Rex got up. Every time John hitched Rex to the buggy he threw himself to the ground, and every time Uncle Will tied him to the tractor he got up and walked, but he would not pull the buggy. At last he broke the buggy shafts. Finally, in desperation John led Rex home. He had won the battle and sealed his fate. He was butchered and used to make dog food.

"Well, we lost money on that deal," said Father. "I could have sold him as untrained as the other owner had, but this way I have a clear conscience."

One night after that episode with Rex and the tractor, Edith heard the hum of a tractor in her sleep, and it seemed to be suffocating her. The noise hurt her head as she fought sleep. As soon as she was partly awake she realized that the motor was not outside. It was inside and on her bed. It was the cat purring contently and rubbing its soft furry body against Edith's head, this being the only part of her that was available.

"How in the world did you get in the house?" Edith asked out loud, for cats and dogs were not allowed in the house. The only answer was a pleased purring and more head rubbing.

"Stop it," Edith scolded, for she did not like to be disturbed from a sound sleep at midnight. The cat was too happy to notice Edith's lack of enthusiasm, so Edith got up and opened the one window that had a porch roof under it, and threw out the cat, none too gently.

She sighed peacefully as she lay down again. Her suffocating headache was already disappearing. Her relief was short-lived, for in a few minutes the cat was back, purring and rubbing its hot furry body against Edith's head.

Edith just was not in the mood for love, she wanted sleep. She threw the cat out on the roof again. This time she hollered, "Floyd, close your window. The cat is coming in your window, across your room, through the spare room, through the hall and into my bedroom." Edith heard the noise of a screen being put in the window. The cat did not return.

Chapter 21

Autumn Work

*e*very year Father planted a big field of corn. The fodder from this corn was used to feed the steers during the winter months. The corn was used as grain to feed the hens and other farm animals.

Every fall the men cut down the corn stalks and tied them into upright bundles of shocks. The whole field of corn was cut into shocks and left to dry.

Early on damp days or frosty mornings, Father tore down four shocks at a time. He laid these on the ground in a large square, one shock in each corner. Then he pulled all the ears of corn from two shocks and Edith did the same with her two shocks. They husked the corn as they pulled them off their shocks. They tossed the husked ears of corn into the center of the square on the ground.

Corn could be husked only when the weather was damp and cold or the corn was wet with heavy dew. The fodder gave off a musky wet odor that was very pleasing to Edith. She loved to pretend that the big yellow corn was a roaring campfire and she was lost in the woods and only survived because she had that fire. Sometimes, when Edith was deep in her daydreams, the corn actually seemed to throw heat at Edith's cold body. At other times, it was just a plain pile of corn.

There were other fun chores in the autumn. One chore that was very pleasant was picking huckleberries in the mountains. They started getting ready the evening before they wanted to leave. Father laid out the feed for the horses and cows. He put the right amount of corn and wheat in the bucket for the hens, and filled their feeders with mash. He filled the trough with water for the horses and he gave extra buckets of water for the hens so Mother could do all the chores by herself. She was the only one that would stay at home with Emma and Alice. She had to do all the men's chores, and do the work in the house as well.

Edith was too excited to sleep that night. She tried repeating the multiplication table, up to and including the twelfth. She finished and was still wide-awake. So she tried repeating it backwards. That did not help either. Then she started all over with the second table.

The next thing she knew Father was calling her. "Edith, time to get up. We are going for huckleberries this morning, remember?" but Edith was too heavy with sleep to answer. "Edith, are you awake?" Father called again.

"Huh," was all that Edith could mutter.

"Edith, do you hear me? We are going for huckleberries this morning." Slowly, the message began to take hold of Edith's senses.

"Yes, Father, I am coming," she answered. In another minute she was up and searching for her clothing in the dark.

It was only three o'clock in the morning, but Father wanted an early start. They needed to pick enough berries to last until next year. Everybody hurried. The cows had never been milked so quickly before, nor the other chores done so swiftly. In fact, the family was in the house before Mother had breakfast on the table. After they had said their silent grace and ate a hurried breakfast, Mother handed Father a picnic lunch she had prepared for the family.

The spring wagon had only one seat, but it had a bed, (like a pick-up truck had) and it was filled with tubs; buckets and lard cans to be filled with berries. There was also a container with a handle for each member of the group. Edith had to move some containers to make space so she could sit beside Henry. She wanted to talk.

A few stars were shining dimly, but most of them were shrouded in fog. As soon as Jerry was limbered up a bit, Father urged him to a trot. The wagon lantern shed a shadowy light across Jerry's back and the night breeze fanned Edith's face. In the distance a roaster crowed, then only the crickets were heard. Jerry's hooves clip-clopped on the road. It was a ghostly sound in a ghostly white world. It was eerie.

Then a rabbit suddenly appeared out of the mist, for a moment, and was gone. Edith was not even sure that she had seen it.

"That was a ghost rabbit," whispered Henry. "Didn't you see his long ears?"

"It was just a rabbit," Edith whispered back.

"Then why are you whispering?" whispered Henry. The trees looked ghostly too, with their misty white leaves that faded into the background of fog.

"Everybody is fast asleep," whispered Henry. "We are the only people that know we are alive." It was scary. Now and then a dim light appeared at some window, but it too was shrouded in mist. Slowly, the fog lifted and the light that shone at the windows looked more natural. Edith breathed a sigh of relief. Then they saw another rabbit.

"That ghost rabbit is following us," whispered Henry. "He is going to get us," but Edith refused to be drawn under that ghostly spell again—besides daylight was fast approaching.

They were passing more houses with lighted windows now. When they gazed to the east, the sun was beginning to divide the fog and darkness from the light. Then, there was no darkness. Soon the streets filled with speeding cars. All of a sudden the rest of the world had risen to greet the new day.

It took a little over an hour to get to Churchtown, where Fannie, Father's oldest daughter lived, with her husband, Sam Sauder. This was the family's first stop. Soon Fannie and Sam were ready to join the merry group of berry pickers. Sam knew where the best huckleberry patches were. Every year he guided Father to these patches.

The Sauders picked huckleberries in a woody patch near their farm.
Whenever time permitted, they gathered
the huckleberries that grew in that patch
and the surrounding area. Consequently,
they had lots of berries preserved by
the time the Fox family arrived in late
summer. For this reason, every bucket
Fannie and Sam picked, they poured
into one of Father's containers. Sam was
such a fast picker that Edith marveled at
the ease with which he filled bucket after
bucket.

Huckleberries

Most of the day Edith skirted the group of pickers.
She found she surprised more wildlife if she was not in the
group's midst. She stopped often to admire lovely wild flowers.
There were strange plants to see, and stranger butterflies and
moths to admire. She surprised rabbits and squirrels from their
hiding places. Pheasants and quails flew up in front of her,
nearly scaring her out of her wits. She found unpicked huckleberry bushes laden with berries so ripe that they almost fell
into her bucket. Other bushes had been picked empty or had
only a few berries left. Now and then, Father called everyone's
name to make sure no one was lost.

It was all so wonderful and exciting Edith could hardly
believe it was time to eat, when Father called everyone together
for lunch. When they began to eat their sandwiches, Edith discovered she was hungry.

Father was pleased when he saw how many containers
were nearly full. This was a good huckleberry year. They would
have lots of huckleberry pies this winter.

"We will pick a few more hours, then we must head
for home. Mother has to sort the berries tonight, so she can
get an early start to can them tomorrow morning. We have to

get home before nightfall, and get the chores done," observed Father. "Mother can not do the milking by herself."

They were ready to leave the mountains a few hours later. Edith was tired, but happy as she climbed into the wagon. On the way home they dropped the Sauders off at their home.

"Thank you much for helping us and giving us all your berries. We sure appreciate it," said Father.

"We are so happy that you ask us to join you. We look forward to this day every year," was the reply.

The hour-long drive relaxed Edith's tired body, so she was ready to help with the milking when they arrived at the farm. She was ready for bed at an early hour, however.

Chapter 22

Grown-up

I t was a lazy Sunday afternoon. Edith and Alice were sitting in the shade of the porch, where a faint breeze fanned them.

In the maple tree above their heads, the Baltimore oriole's hanging nest rocked gently in the breeze. The parent birds were flying back and forth with insects to feed their hungry young. When the parents neared the nest a frantic chirping began and open mouths appeared above the rim of the nest.

"They are really noisy," Alice observed.

"They are saying, I am hungry, feed me first," Edith explained.

"I don't care what they are saying," Alice angrily exclaimed. "I am tired of watching them. I wish somebody would come home."

"It will be at least three more hours before Father, Mother and Emma come home. Funerals take long, you know. You don't want the boys to come home. They will just fight with us."

But Alice refused to be satisfied. "I don't care. I am tired of sitting here doing nothing." Alice still had problems sitting still even if it was just for five minutes.

"I want to go over to the quarry," she decided then.

"In this heat?"

"I don't care. I am tired of sitting."

Young David lived in a lane on the farm that Father had bought after that strange walk that had Edith puzzled so much. Behind these farm buildings, a lane led to a large hole in the earth. This hole had been a stone quarry a long time ago. The rock had all been removed, and the opening was now being filled with garbage. Most of this refuse came from overstocked stores and garment factories. Rooting through junk produced many cherished items, proving the age-old saying that one person's junk is another person's treasure. The neighborhood children enjoyed this hunting for hidden treasure too.

Edith and Alice set out for the stone quarry with bare feet burning on the hot road surface. When they turned in the lane, they dug their toes in the soft dust, avoiding the stony places.

As soon as they arrived at the quarry, Edith saw they had made a mistake. "We forgot our shoes. We'll have to go back and get them."

"It's too hot." Alice brushed her brow with her hand. "We can just take care that we don't step on anything sharp." But Alice did not follow her own advice. A moment later she cried, "Ouch! Ouch! Ouch! I am hurt!"

When Edith turned, Alice was holding her foot in the air. Blood was dripping from it.

"Now, what did you do."

"I stepped on a piece of broken glass," Alice wailed. Edith helped her back to the grassy bank, where she sat down.

"I don't know what to do with you," Edith said.

"Maybe Davids are home."

"They're not. The blinds were pulled down when we passed."

"Then what will you do?" Alice began a loud wailing.

"Shut up, so I can think." Alice quieted down immediately. "I can't let you here, you'll bleed to death." Alice started sobbing again, and Edith knew she had said the wrong thing. "Shut up," she hollered again. Then in a softer tone of voice, she asked, "Can you walk?"

"No, I am bleeding."

"Then I'll have to carry you."

"You can't, I am too big."

"Well then, can you walk?"

"No."

"Then I will have to carry you. I have no choice." Alice was very heavy. Edith could hardly carry her. When she thought she could not go another step, she would see the blood dripping from Alice's foot. It gave her the incentive she needed to take another step. That was the longest one-fourth mile Edith had ever walked. Finally, she got Alice home and on the settee in the kitchen.

"I'll have to find something to bandage that foot," she told Alice. She hurried to the closet, where the bed sheets were kept. She took a sheet and tore it into strips.

There was a puddle of blood on the floor by this time. Edith did not look at it. She just began to wrap that foot. The blood seeped through as fast as she wrapped. She wrapped and wrapped. Alice's foot looked like a balloon, but the blood no longer oozed through the bandage.

"Lay down and keep perfectly still," Edith commanded, and for once Alice was willing to lie quietly. She fell asleep. Edith sat on the floor beside her, watching for signs of more bleeding. She fell asleep.

She awoke with a start, when she heard the screen door slam. "What happened? What is all this blood doing on the floor?" It was Mother, and she was concerned.

Edith had been too tired to clean the floor, but now she explained it all to Mother, while Emma stood there speechless.

"You carried your sister home from the quarry! She is almost as heavy as you are!"

"She seemed much heavier," Edith told her. Mother took care of Alice's foot properly, and then she turned to Edith.

"I can see that you are a big girl now. The way you took care of Alice. You did a good job of bandaging that foot too, so she did not lose too much blood."

Edith looked at Mother in surprise. "You mean I am a grown-up now?"

"That is exactly what I mean."

Edith just stood there. "Wow," she said. Then "Wow," again. "But you always know everything. I didn't know what to do. I was scared."

"So are we many times, but we do something anyway, which is exactly what you did. You saved Alice from losing a lot of blood. That was a very grown-up thing to do."

Edith stood there and smiled. Everything had turned out all right. Alice's foot healed nicely too. This being a grown-up was just as wonderful as she had expected it to be.

But when had it all happened. Her mind flashed back through the years, when she had told Lydia she wanted to be a grown-up.

"But then you will have to work," Lydia had told her.

"Then I will like to work," she had predicted, and it had all come true. She loved to go berry picking. She loved to feed the baby chicks. She loved to husk corn in autumn. Baking cookies and washing dishes was not nearly as bad as it used to be. It was rather nice to clean the kitchen too; everything was so bright and shiny afterward.

She also remembered when John asked her to go along to church in his new top buggy. And she had been invited to Uncle Will's daughter's wedding, and there were many other signs that she had missed. How could she have missed them all?

"I may be grown-up," she told herself, "but, now I have to learn how to be more observant."